Praise for the Kiss, Bow, or Shake Hands *series*

"In this global economy, ANYONE who leaves the U.S. is a fool if they don't read up on their destination's customs. *Kiss, Bow, or Shake Hands* is THE definitive authority on how to conduct yourself around the world. You can easily offend your prospects and there is no faster way to kill the most lucrative business deal. *Kiss, Bow, or Shake Hands* has been immeasurably helpful over the years."

—Louis Altman, President, New Hampshire International
Trade Association (NHITA), and President, GlobaFone

"*Kiss, Bow, or Shake Hands* has been an invaluable resource for international businesspeople for years. Don't leave home without it."

—Joe Douress, Vice President,
LexisNexis Martindale-Hubbell

"*Kiss, Bow, or Shake Hands* is a great resource of cultural and business-related information. The material is concise and easy to read. The cultural information is unique, educational, and fun! It's a book that can be enjoyed by a great number of people, from a student, to a leisure traveler, to the most sophisticated business person."

—Joanna Savvides, President,
World Trade Center of Greater Philadelphia

"In my work, I train employees of multinational corporations on how to manage the intercultural aspects of an international assignment. *Kiss, Bow, or Shake Hands* is a tremendous resource for the growing number of individuals in today's global workforce who find themselves working across international borders and on assignment outside their home country."

—Carolyn Ryffel, Senior Manager of Intercultural Services,
Cartus, Chicago, IL

"To help achieve success in communicating globally about our business, there are critical tools never far from my reach: my laptop or BlackBerry, my phone, and Terri Morrison's *Kiss, Bow, or Shake Hands*."

—Sherry Nebel, Vice President–Communications,
Connexion by Boeing

KISS, BOW, OR SHAKE HANDS:

How to Do Business in
12 Asian Countries

ASIA

- CULTURAL OVERVIEWS
- TIPS FOR DOING BUSINESS • KNOW BEFORE YOU GO
- NEGOTIATING STRATEGIES
- PROTOCOL

TERRI MORRISON AND WAYNE A. CONAWAY

AVON, MASSACHUSETTS

To Nica, Brendan, and Alex
Forever Wise, Forever True, Forever Loved
And to Tony
A chuisle mochroí
—TERRI MORRISON

To my Parents
I hope I was a good long-term investment.
—WAYNE A. CONAWAY

And to the late George A. Borden, Ph.D.,
a gifted friend.

This book includes material previously published in *Kiss, Bow, or Shake Hands* by
Terri Morrison, © 2006, F+W Publications, Inc.

Published by Adams Media, an F+W Publications Company
57 Littlefield Street
Avon, MA 02322
www.adamsmedia.com

ISBN 10: 1-59869-216-X
ISBN 13: 978-1-59869-216-7

Printed in the United States of America.

J I H G F E D C B A

Library of Congress Cataloging-in-Publication Data
is available from publisher.

Maps © Map Resouces.

This book is available at quantity discounts for bulk purchases.
For information, please call 1-800-289-0963.

Contents

Preface

IN THE DOZEN YEARS since the first edition of *Kiss, Bow, or Shake Hands* was originally published, Asia has changed in remarkable ways. Asian economies grew, collapsed, and recovered. The region coped with epidemics, earthquakes, and tsunamis. Indonesia went from one-party rule to democracy. Vietnam, once a pariah to the USA and its allies, transformed itself into a valued trading partner. India became the outsourcing capital of the world. The Soviet Union dissolved, leaving its Central Asian republics to find a new path alone. Japan slowed, and China boomed. The interesting thing is that over twelve years—throughout all of the massive political and economic changes—the cultures, values, and belief systems of major ethnic groups have remained constant.

For example, the former British Crown Colony of Hong Kong was returned to China in 1997. After decades under British rule, the businesspeople of Hong Kong had to adapt to the rules of the People's Republic of China. Many multinationals will grapple with the written and unwritten rules of conduct in China as well (like Google, which was temporarily censored by the Chinese government for several days in 2006). Successful globalization will require that you, too, learn how to adapt to the cultural aspects of doing business in Asia.

Just understanding Chinese name order and titles will give you an advantage over other executives who do no research.

As Johann Wolfgang von Goethe said, "There is nothing more terrible than ignorance in action" *(Es ist nichts schrecklicher als eine tätige Unwissenheit).*

During my life, I have seen World War, reconstruction, terrorism, and tremendous advances in technology. On this increasingly interconnected planet, businesses need to acknowledge that people are not alike all over the world—the more you respect local attitudes toward families, work, and religion, the more successful you will be in those locales. Priorities in Mumbai are not necessarily equivalent to those in Milwaukee.

It is a pleasure to introduce you to this important book. Review it before you embark on your international trips. Gain the information you need on business practices, cognitive styles, negotiation techniques, and social customs. Give the right gift; make the right gesture. Read *Kiss, Bow, or Shake Hands: Asia*.

—HANS H.B. KOEHLER,
the former Director of the Wharton Export Network

"The reputation of a thousand years
may be determined by the conduct of one hour."
—JAPANESE PROVERB

Introduction

WHAT WILL YOU NEED TO KNOW in 2010 or 2020 to work in Asia? As Hans Koehler pointed out in his Preface, we live in changing times. In this century China and India are changing the economic balance of the world. But many of the cultural tenets presented in *Kiss, Bow, or Shake Hands: Asia* took hundreds or thousands of years to develop. These stable precepts help us understand why people behave differently around the world, and they will help you to avoid global marketing faux pas like these:

> *McDonald's Corporation settled a group of lawsuits for $10 million in 2002. Why were they sued? Because of their French fries and hash browns. After 1990, McDonald's stated that only pure vegetable oil was used to cook their fries, implying that they were prepared in a "vegetarian" manner. However, the oil contained the essence of beef flavor, which is an anathema to Hindus and vegetarians worldwide. Most of the money from the lawsuit was donated to Hindu and other vegetarian causes.*

> *Nike was forced to recall thousands of pairs of Air Bakin, Air BBQ, Air Grill, and Air Melt shoes because of a decoration intended to resemble fire on the back of the sneakers. Unfortunately, when viewed from right to left (which is the way Arabic is read), the flames resembled the Arabic word for Allah. Muslims saw this as a desecration on two levels: 1) the name of Allah may not be used on a product, and 2) Arabic tradition deems that the foot is unclean. Facing worldwide protests and boycotts, Nike implemented an enormous recall of the expensive sneakers.*

As these examples show, an unintentional misstep can threaten or destroy your costly international marketing efforts. It also illustrates the benefits of learning the language of your target countries, and corroborating translations and design elements locally.

Kiss, Bow, or Shake Hands: Asia is organized in a clear, consistent manner to help you easily find the data you need to avoid many of the errors others have made before you.

The work to develop this volume resulted in not only this book, but much additional information that is available on our Web site, *www.kissboworshakehands.com*. The Web site also contains information on official world holidays, recommendations for learning foreign languages, gift-giving suggestions, legal data, and hundreds of articles like "Subtle Gestures," and "Lie To Me." *Kiss, Bow* is now part of a larger electronic database—*Kiss, Bow, or Shake Hands: Expanded Edition*. You are always welcome to contact us at 610-725-1040 or e-mail *TerriMorrison@getcustoms.com* with your questions or comments.

Each chapter in this book focuses on a single country, and all are organized into sections, such as in the following example for China:

What's Your Cultural IQ?
Three quick questions to gauge your knowledge

Tips on Doing Business in China
Five business-related highlights

Country Background
Demographics, History, Type of Government, Language, and The Chinese View (perspectives from the country's viewpoint)

Know Before You Go
Natural and human hazards

Cultural Orientation
A cultural anthropologist's view. This section is described in detail in an introductory chapter.

Business Practices
Punctuality, Appointments, and Local Time; Negotiating; Business Entertaining

Protocol
Greetings, Titles/Forms of Address, Gestures, Gifts, and Dress

And many Cultural Notes on a variety of subjects are scattered throughout the chapters.

(For more details on Titles/Forms of Address, Mailing Addresses, etc., we recommend an excellent book called *Merriam-Webster's Guide to International Business Communications*, by Toby D. Atkinson.)

Please remember that you will work with individuals, and there are always exceptions to every rule. For example, *Kiss, Bow* suggests that many Japanese executives are reserved, polite, quiet, and rarely display emotion. Somewhere there is probably a loud, boisterous, gesticulating Japanese manager who is as emotional and imperious as any prima donna. Just because we haven't met him (or her) doesn't mean that no such person exists.

The process of communication is fluid, not static. The success of your intercultural interactions depends upon you and the quality of your information. *Kiss, Bow, or Shake Hands: Asia* provides you with the best and most current data possible on what foreign business and social practices to expect in your efforts at globalization.

"Audi alteram partem."
—Hear the other side.

Cultural Orientation

FOR EACH OF THE COUNTRIES in *Kiss, Bow, or Shake Hands: Asia* there is a Cultural Orientation section. The study of cultural orientation gives us a model for understanding and predicting the results of intercultural encounters. It is, however, a model—a theory. New discoveries continue to be made about why we act the way we do.

Furthermore, communication always takes place between individuals, not cultures. Few individuals are perfect representations of their culture. Citizens of the United States of America are generally known for addressing one another by first names, a habit that most of the world does not follow. However, there are many U.S. citizens who are more comfortable with formality, and prefer to use last names and titles. This does not make them any less like U.S. citizens. It just makes them individuals.

Many global executives adopt the manners of their targeted countries, so why do U.S. executives need to study foreign ways? There are a variety of reasons.

First of all, many foreign businesspeople often cannot or will not imitate U.S. mannerisms. Can you afford to leave them out of your business plans?

Second, you might wish to sell to the general public in a foreign market. The average foreign consumer is certainly not going to have the same habits or tastes as consumers in the United States of America.

Third, although your business counterpart in Japan may act or speak like an American or Canadian or Australian at times, he isn't. He probably is not even thinking in English; he is thinking in Japanese. Knowing how Japanese people tend to arrive at decisions gives you an edge. And don't we all need every business advantage we can get?

Following the cultural orientation section, there is a breakdown of the information contained therein.

Cognitive Styles: How We Organize and Process Information

The word "cognitive" refers to thought, so "cognitive styles" refers to thought patterns. We take in data every conscious moment. Some of it is just noise, and we ignore it. Some of it is of no interest, and we forget it as soon as we see/hear/feel/smell/taste it. Some data, however, we choose to accept.

Open-minded or Closed-minded?

Studies of cognitive styles suggest that people fall into *open-minded* and *closed-minded* categories. The open-minded person seeks out more information before making a decision. The closed-minded person has tunnel vision—he or she sees only a narrow range of data and ignores the rest.

Something that might surprise you is that most experts in cultural orientation consider the citizens of the USA and Canada to be closed-minded.

Open-minded people are more apt to see the relativity of issues. They admit that they don't have all the answers, and that they need to learn before they can come to a proper conclusion. Frankly, there are not many cultures like that. Most cultures produce closed-minded citizens.

Here's an example: Most theocratic (governed by religious leaders) cultures are closed-minded. That's one of the characteristics of such a culture: God tells you what is important. Anything outside of those parameters can be ignored. From a business point of view, that can be a weakness. For example, Islam prohibits charging interest on a loan. There can be no argument and no appeal: Charging interest is wrong. Obviously, running a modern banking system without charging interest is challenging.

So why are Canada and the USA closed-minded?

Assume that someone from an Islamic country tells a North American that the United States of America is evil and should become a theocracy. The North American is likely to scoff. The United States a theocracy? Nonsense! Why, the separation of church and state is one of the most sacred precepts established by the founding fathers of the United States of America.

That North American is being closed-minded. He or she is refusing to even consider the Muslim's reasoning. A truly open-minded person would consider the proposition. He or she might reject the possibility after due thought, but not without a complete evaluation.

In fact, a person who wants to study cultural orientation should consider such questions. Granted, most businesspeople would probably decide that the United States of America should not become a theocracy. But considering the topic can lead to some useful insights. Perhaps most important is the concept that much of the world does not share the United States' predilection for the separation of church and state. This separation is a specifically Western notion, which evolved out of the hundreds of years of European religious wars that followed the Protestant Reformation.

In point of fact, most cultures tend to produce closed-minded citizens as long as things are working fairly well. It often takes a major disaster to make people open-minded. For example, the citizens of many former Communist nations are now becoming open-minded. Their old Communist ideology has fallen apart, and they realize they need new answers.

Associative or Abstractive Thinking?

Another aspect of cognitive styles is how people process information. We divide such processing into *associative* and *abstractive* characteristics.

A person who thinks associatively is filtering new data through the screen of personal experience. New data (we'll call it X) can only be understood in relation to similar past experiences (Is this new X more like A, or maybe B?). What if X is not like anything ever encountered before? The associative thinker is still going to pigeonhole that new data in with something else (X is just another B). On the other hand, the abstractive thinker can deal with something genuinely new. When the abstractive person encounters new data, he or she doesn't have to lump it in with past experiences (It's not A, it's not B or C—it's new! It's X!). The abstractive person is more able to extrapolate data and consider hypothetical situations ("I've never experienced X, but I've read about how such things might occur").

Obviously, no country has more than its share of smart (or dull) people. However, some cultures have come to value abstractive thinking, whereas others encourage associative patterns. Much of this has to do with the educational system. A system that teaches by rote tends to produce associative thinkers. An educational system that teaches problem-solving develops abstractive thinking. The scientific method is very much a product of abstractive thinking. Both northern Europe and North America produce a lot of abstractive thinkers.

Particular or Universal Thinking?

One final category has to do with how thinking and behavior are focused. People are divided into *particular* versus *universal* thinkers. The particularistic person feels that a personal relationship is more important than obeying rules or laws. On the other hand, the universalistic person tends to obey regulations and laws; relationships are less important than an individual's duty to the company, society, and authority in general.

Not surprisingly, the previous categories tend to go together in certain patterns. Abstractive thinkers often display universalistic behavior: It requires abstractive thought to see beyond one's personal relationships and consider "the good of society" (which is a very abstract concept).

Negotiation Strategies: What We Accept as Evidence

In general, let us assume that everyone acts on the basis of his or her own best interests. The question becomes: How do I decide if this is a good deal or not? Or, in a broader sense, what is the truth?

Different cultures arrive at truth in different ways. These ways can be distilled into *faith*, *facts*, and *feelings*.

The person who acts on the basis of faith is using a belief system, which can be a religious or political ideology. For example, many small nations believe in self-sufficiency. They may reject a deal that is overwhelmingly advantageous simply because they want their own people to do it. It doesn't matter that you can provide a better-quality product at a much lower price; they believe it is better that their fellow citizens produce the product, even if they produce an inferior product at a higher cost. Presenting facts to such a person is a waste of time. His or her faith operates independently from facts.

Clearly, people who believe in facts want to see evidence to support your position. They can be the most predictable to work with. If you offer the low bid, you get the job.

People who believe in feelings are the most common throughout the world. These are the people who "go with their gut instincts." They need to like you in order to do business with you. It can take a long time to build up a relationship with them. However, once that relationship is established, it is very strong. They aren't going to run to the first company that undercuts your offer.

Value Systems: The Basis for Behavior

Each culture has a system for dividing right from wrong, or good from evil. After a general statement concerning the values of the culture, this section identifies the culture's three value systems (Locus of Decision-Making, Sources of Anxiety Reduction, and Issues of Equality/Inequality). These following three sections identify the Value Systems in the predominant culture of each country.

Locus of Decision-Making

This section explores how much a culture prizes individualism as opposed to collectivism. Some countries, such as the USA, are very individualistic, while others, such as China, are very collectivistic. A person in the United States may consider only himself or herself when making a decision, while a person in China must abide by the consensus of the collective group.

Such pure individualism and collectivism is rare. In most countries people consider more than just themselves, but are not bound by the desires of the group.

It is possible to consider the loci of decision-making as a series of concentric circles. In the center, in the smallest circle, is the individual. The next circle, slightly larger, is usually the family. Many cultures expect each individual to consider "What is best for my family?" prior to making any decisions. The next circle represents a larger group. It could be an ethnic group, a religion, or even the individual's country. Some cultures expect individuals to consider the best interests of the entire, expansive group.

Of course, when a person is acting as representative for a company, the best interests of the company may be paramount.

Sources of Anxiety Reduction

Every human being on this planet is subject to stress. How do we handle it? How do we reduce anxiety?

We can identify four basic sources of security and stability that people turn to: interpersonal relationships, religion, technology, and the law. Frequently, a combination of sources is used.

A person who must decide on an important business deal is under stress. If this person is your client, it may help you to know where he or she will turn for help and advice. This is especially true when the person turns to interpersonal relationships. If an executive is going to ask his or her spouse for advice, you had better make sure that you have made a good impression on that spouse.

Issues of Equality/Inequality

An important characteristic of all cultures is the division of power. Who controls the government, and who controls the business resources?

"All men are created equal" is a sacred tenet of the United States of America. Despite this, prejudice against many groups still exists in the United States.

All cultures have disadvantaged groups. This section identifies some sectors that have unequal status. These can be defined by economic status as well as by race or gender. Only the most industrialized nations tend to have a large, stable middle class. Many countries have a small, rich elite and a huge, poverty-stricken underclass.

Issues of male-female equality are also analyzed in this section. It is useful for a female business executive to know how women are regarded in a foreign country.

Never forget that this model represents cultural patterns that may or may not apply to each individual you contact and get to know. Utilize this information as a guideline and remain open to the new experiences we all encounter abroad.

> "*Vérité en-deça des Pyrénées, erreur au-delà.*"
> —BLAISE PASCAL, 1623–1662

> "There are truths on this side of the Pyrenees which are falsehoods on the other."
> —TRANSLATION: GEERT HOFSTEDE

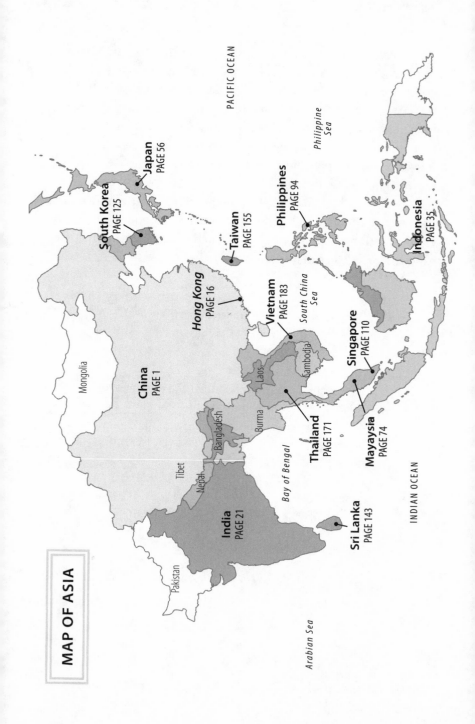

MAP OF ASIA

Mongolia

Tibet

Nepal

Pakistan

Bangladesh

Burma

Laos

Cambodia

PACIFIC OCEAN

Philippine Sea

South China Sea

Bay of Bengal

Arabian Sea

INDIAN OCEAN

China

People's Republic of China
Local short form: Zhong Guo
Local long form: Zhonghua Renmin Gongheguo
Abbreviation: PRC

Cultural Note

The People's Republic of China is well on its way to becoming the superpower of the twenty-first century. Aside from having the world's largest population and the world's largest army, it is a nuclear and space power. Now it is a global economic power as well. In February of 2005, the government of China lent the government of Russia U.S. $6 billion to help Moscow nationalize the oil company Yukos.

▶ WHAT'S YOUR CULTURAL IQ?

1. TRUE or FALSE? The Chinese are not interested in most international sports.
   ANSWER: FALSE. While many Chinese have limited experience playing sports, they are often avid fans (and sports gamblers). When Shanghai-born Yao Ming joined the Houston Rockets in 2002, Chinese interest in basketball soared overnight. And the Beijing Olympics has generated massive interest in Olympic sports.

2. Match the following Nobel Prize laureates with the appropriate prize:
   a. Tenzin Gyatso   1. Nobel in physics, 1957
   b. Chen Ning Yang   2. Nobel for literature, 2000
   c. Gao Xingjian   3. Nobel Peace Prize, 1989
   ANSWERS: a. 3; b. 1; c. 2. Tenzin Gyatso is better known as the fourteenth Dalai Lama of Tibet. Tibet, of course, has been occupied by the PRC since 1950. Gao Xingjian was the first Chinese to win the Nobel for literature. There have been many Nobel Prizes awarded to Chinese in

the sciences, although most of the recipients (like Chen Ning Yang) have done their most important scientific work in the West.

3. There are many places in Asia where the People's Republic of China finds itself in conflict with other countries. Which of these is *not* currently an international "hot spot?"
   a. Macao
   b. North Korea
   c. The Spratly Islands
   d. Taiwan

ANSWER: a. Portugal ceded its colony of Macao to the PRC at the end of 1999, and Macao has been relatively peaceful since then. A traditional site for gambling, Macao is the only place on the Chinese mainland where casinos are permitted.

▶ TIPS ON DOING BUSINESS IN CHINA

- Experienced travelers avow that patience is the most important skill needed to do business in China. The Chinese are very good at figuring out when a foreigner is under pressure from a tight deadline, and they turn that to their advantage in negotiations.
- Although the economic boom is changing things, China is still a hierarchical society. Age is respected. When you send more than one representative to China, the oldest person should receive deference from the younger ones. The elder representative should even enter and leave the conference room first.
- While the Chinese have made great strides in using the Internet, they face serious obstacles. For one thing, the thousands of ideographs in Chinese language are not easily adapted to use on a computer keyboard. Also, Internet use in China is hampered by the government, which censors Web sites and periodically shuts down Internet cafés.
- If possible, avoid traveling to China during the lunar New Year. Also called Spring Festival, this is China's most important, nationwide weeklong holiday. Tradition demands that every Chinese return to his or her traditional home during the lunar New Year. With so many migrants to the cities, this means that there are

millions of trips taken by car, bus, train, or airplane during the festival.

Cultural Note

The lunar New Year puts enormous strains on China's transportation infrastructure. Many people wait for days just to secure standing room on a train or bus. To alleviate this, the Chinese government is considering mandating staggered vacations, in the hope that travel will be eased if not everyone is off work at the same time. This may ease travel during China's other national holidays, but it is doubtful whether it will eliminate the Spring Festival tradition of returning to one's ancestral home.

▶ COUNTRY BACKGROUND

Demographics
China has 1.3 billion inhabitants (2006 estimate), making it the most populous country in the world. One quarter of the earth's population lives there. Although there are many minority groups, over 91 percent of the population is ethnic (Han) Chinese. China has implemented a rigorous birth control program that limits couples to only one child.

History
The Chinese boast the world's oldest continuous civilization, with more than 4,000 years of recorded history. Beijing (old Peking) has been the capital of China for over 800 years and is the country's political, economic, and cultural hub.

China was ruled by strong dynasties for thousands of years. The first recorded dynasty, the Hsia, existed around 2200 B.C., and the last dynasty, the Ch'ing, ended in 1911. Some of the most important cultural achievements in history were produced during this time, such as papermaking, the compass, gunpowder, and movable-type printing.

After the fall of the last dynasty, Sun Yat-sen founded the Republic of China and was succeeded by Chiang Kai-shek in 1927.

Mao Tse-tung's Communist forces took control in 1949 and established the Communist government that still exists, although events—

from the massacre in Tiananmen Square in June of 1989 on—have shown an increasingly popular demand for democratic reform.

China has been divided into twenty-two provinces, five autonomous regions, and three municipalities.

Type of Government

The People's Republic of China has a Communist government. There is a single legislative house, the National People's Congress; all members belong to the Communist Party. The National People's Congress elects the Standing Committee, which holds executive power and is made up of the premier and leading ministers. The premier is the head of the government; the president is the chief of state. The position of secretary general of the Central Committee of the Chinese Communist Party is also an office of great power; it is often held by the current president.

The Communist regime is highly centralized and authoritarian, and controls many aspects of life in China.

Current government data can be found at the Embassy of China at *www.china-embassy.org.*

Cultural Note

The revolutionary government of the People's Republic of China made changes to the Chinese language. Many complex symbols in written Chinese were simplified. And the direction of written Chinese was changed: instead of being written in vertical columns, it is now primarily written like most Western tongues, from left to right in horizontal rows.

This reformed Chinese has not been universally accepted by the Chinese outside the PRC. Some Taiwanese refuse to reform Chinese, preferring the pre-revolutionary forms. When you go to the PRC, make sure your translators use reformed Chinese.

Language

The official national language is standard Chinese, based on the Mandarin dialect. It is spoken by more than 70 percent of the population. Many Chinese speak Cantonese, Shanghainese, and Kejia dialects. Ethnologue, at *www.ethnologue.com*, recognizes 202 languages.

Each minority speaks its own dialect or language. English is spoken by many businesspeople.

Although spoken Chinese has many dialects (some of which are as different as English is from German) there is one common written language. This is why many Chinese movies include Chinese sub-titles, so that Cantonese-speaking Chinese audiences can understand the Mandarin-speaking actors, or vice versa.

The government of the PRC has begun investing in Chinese language training for foreigners. Contributions to support Chinese language programs are being made to major trade partners worldwide.

Cultural Note

Of all its trading partners, China's relationship with Japan is one of its most contradictory. The government of the PRC is always ready to criticize Japan for any real or imagined offense, from Japan's cozy relationship with Taiwan to Japan's failure to be properly abashed for its military actions in China before and during the Second World War. Yet, in 2004, China surpassed the USA as Japan's largest trading partner. Their trade continues, despite such real conflicts as both countries claiming the same offshore oil fields, or a Chinese submarine being detected in Japanese waters in November of 2004.

The Chinese View

Despite the fact that the government encourages atheism, the Chinese Constitution guarantees religious freedom (within certain constraints). Buddhism, Islam, and Christianity are the three major formal religions practiced in China. However, even larger numbers of Chinese believe in traditional Chinese philosophies, notably Confucianism and Taoism.

Confucianism, although not a religion with a divine deity, has great influence on Chinese society. Confucius was a Chinese scholar and statesman who lived during feudal times over 2,000 years ago. He established a rigid ethical and moral system that governs all relationships.

Confucius taught that the basic unit of society is the family. In order to preserve harmony in the home, certain reciprocal responsibilities must be preserved in relationships. These relationships are between ruler and subjects, between husband and wife, between father and son, between elder brother and younger brother, and between friends. Since all but the last are hierarchal, rank and age have historically been very important in all interactions. All actions of the individual reflect upon the family, and filial devotion is of utmost importance. The virtues of kindness, propriety, righteousness, intelligence, and faithfulness have also been deeply revered.

☑ Know Before You Go

Most foreign businesspeople in China's major cities will find an environment comparable to that of any city in the industrially developed world. The greatest hazards are from traffic and environmental pollution.

China's less-developed areas present greater challenges. The transportation infrastructure is overloaded, and some foreign goods (including medicines) may not be readily available.

China is thought to be the source for many forms of influenza that eventually infect people all over the world. It is theorized that this happens not just because of China's unsurpassed population density, but because of Chinese farming techniques, which allow animals of different species to come into close contact. This is believed to facilitate viral transfer between species, eventually resulting in a virus which infects humans. Certainly, anyone who has visited an outdoor Chinese market will see different species of live animals on sale. The Chinese government recently prohibited such markets from selling civet cats, which were suspected to be the source of the SARS virus.

China is a huge nation, subject to all manner of natural hazards. Earthquakes have caused widespread deaths in the past, but China also suffers from typhoons and other dangerous storms, floods, and mudslides.

Cultural Note

Rural areas in China may have limited accommodations, as well as dangers not usually associated with industrialized nations. For example, schistosomiasis (snail fever) has recently been reported in lakes in Hunan province. A debilitating disease—deadly if not treated—it is caused by a waterborne parasite and can infect humans who come into contact with tainted water for as little as ten seconds. Estimates of the number of people infected run as high as 900,000. Sadly, schistosomiasis was nearly eradicated in China in the 1950s. The return of the disease reflects China's neglect of the countryside in favor of its flourishing cities.

⊙ CULTURAL ORIENTATION

Cognitive Styles: How the Chinese Organize and Process Information

The Chinese are generally circumspect toward outside sources of information. They usually process data through a subjective perspective, derived from experience—unless they have been educated at a Western university. Universalistic behavior that follows the Communist Party line is still required under the Communist government. The favoritism shown to members of the Communist Party is overtly particularistic.

Negotiation Strategies: What the Chinese Accept as Evidence

In general, truth is subjective, and one's feelings, along with a modified belief in the Communist Party line, are primary sources of the truth. Facts are accepted by younger Chinese, particularly within the burgeoning entrepreneurial sector. However, they still strongly consider the other two sources, and will not usually accept a proposal if it is in conflict with their personal feelings for the prospect.

Value Systems: The Basis for Behavior

China is still primarily a collectivistic culture dominated by the Communist Party. The following three sections identify the Value Systems in the predominant culture—their methods of dividing right from wrong, good from evil, and so forth.

Locus of Decision-Making

In a centrally controlled economy, responsibility rests with government planners, but individuals are held responsible for their decisions within the system. Local decisions are made by the head of the collective, and members must behave accordingly. Collectives are insular, closed entities in which individual goals are subordinated to those of the collective. In the zones of free enterprise, businesses are experimenting with freedom from party rule but not from the collectivist way of thinking.

Sources of Anxiety Reduction

The family, school, work unit, and local community are the basic social structures that give stability to a person's life. There is a strong commitment to the extended family. The state, rather than religion, traditionally dictated the standards of wisdom, morality, and the common good. Obedience to parents is integral to a sense of security and stability. Maintaining harmony is vital.

Faith in the Communist Party, which rules the PRC, is abating. Some Chinese look to other ideologies for solace, including native and Western religions, and organizations such as Falun Gong. While most Westerners view Falun Gong as a harmless physical-fitness cult, Beijing has labeled it an "ideological threat." The persecution of Falun Gong demonstrates how ruthlessly the government will attack any rival to its power.

Issues of Equality/Inequality

Relative to the general population (over 1.3 billion), the number of people who are powerful members of the Communist Party is small. There has always been some concern about inequality in a system in which equality is the purpose, but being a member of the party is the only avenue to a position of authority. Free enterprise is purported to breed inequality and uncertainty, but there are rapidly increasing areas where it is allowed to flourish. Age is the only noticeable interpersonal indicator of inequality because it is still revered. Women are purported to be equal to men, but economic and social inequalities continue.

Gender inequality in China also manifests itself in the official "one child" policy. Because a generation of Chinese were only permitted to have one child, many did everything they could to ensure that their child was a boy. Today, China has many more boys than girls, which presents interesting problems when they reach adulthood.

▶ BUSINESS PRACTICES

Punctuality, Appointments, and Local Time

- The work week has generally run from 8:00 A.M. to 5:00 P.M., Monday through Saturday. However, a five-day work week has been initiated in some large cities.

- Punctuality is very important in China, not only for business meetings, but for social occasions as well. Lateness or a cancellation is a serious affront.
- Remember that written Chinese does not have tenses, but there are many words to indicate the passage of time—tomorrow, now, etc.
- Be sure to establish contacts in China before you invest in a trip. Your government's Department of Trade or Commerce can usually assist in arranging appointments with local Chinese business and government officials, and can identify importers, buyers, agents, distributors, and joint venture partners.
- The best times to schedule business trips are April to June and September to October.
- Do not plan business trips during the Chinese New Year, since many businesses close for a week before and after the festival. The date of the New Year varies according to the lunar calendar.
- Be cognizant of the fact that the Chinese write the date differently than most North Americans. The year is written first, then the month, then the day (e.g., December 3, 2010, is written 10.12.03 or 10/12/03).
- China is eight hours ahead of Greenwich Mean Time (G.M.T. + 8), or thirteen hours ahead of U.S. Eastern Standard Time (E.S.T. + 13). Despite the immense size of the country, it has only one time zone.

Negotiating

- Be prepared for the Chinese to supply an interpreter. If possible, bring your own interpreter as well to help you understand nuances in the discussion.
- Avoid slang or jargon, especially figures of speech from sports. Use short, simple sentences, and pause often to make sure that your exact words are understood.
- Expect to make presentations to different groups at different levels.
- Unless you understand the significance of different colors in China, use black and white for your collateral materials.
- Foreign executives—especially those from the USA—have a reputation for impatience, and the Chinese will drag out negotiations well

beyond your deadlines just to gain an advantage. They may try to renegotiate everything on the final day of your visit, and they may continue to try for a better deal even after the contract is signed.

- Never exaggerate your ability to deliver, because the Chinese believe humility is a virtue—and also because they will investigate your claims.
- Chinese may not make any important decisions without first considering whether it is an auspicious day and hour.
- Be patient. Expect to make several trips to China before negotiations are final. The Chinese are cautious in business matters and expect a strong relationship to be built before they close a deal.
- Weights and measures are mainly metric, but several old Chinese measures may still be used.
- Bring business cards with a translation printed (in Mandarin Chinese) on the reverse side. Gold ink is the most prestigious color for the Chinese side. Never place a person's card in your wallet and then put it in your back pocket.
- When entering a business meeting, the highest-ranking member of your group should lead the way.
- The Chinese expect the business conversation to be conducted by the senior officials of each side. Subordinates may speak when they are asked to provide corroborating data, or a comment, but in general, they do not interrupt.
- Familiarize yourself with all aspects of China before you arrive. The Chinese appreciate Western visitors who demonstrate an interest in their culture and history.
- Be patient, expect delays, show little emotion, and do not talk about your deadlines.
- At the end of a meeting, leave before the Chinese.

Business Entertaining
- Business lunches have become popular.
- You will probably be treated to at least one evening banquet. You should always return the favor.
- Banquets at restaurants can be ordered in varying degrees of extravagance. Be sure to reciprocate at the same price per person

as your Chinese host spent at your banquet—never surpass your host in the degree of lavishness.

- Most banquets start between 6:30 and 7:00 P.M. and last for several hours. You should arrive about thirty minutes before your guests—they will arrive on time.
- If you are the guest, always arrive promptly or even a little early.
- Business is not generally discussed during a meal.
- Never begin to eat or drink before your host does.
- When eating rice, it is customary to hold the bowl close to your mouth.
- At a meal, eat lightly in the beginning, as there could be up to twenty courses served. Expect your host to keep filling your bowl with food whenever you empty it. Finishing all of your food may be an insult to your host, because it can mean he did not provide enough food. Leaving a bowl completely full is also rude.
- The Chinese use chopsticks for eating and a porcelain spoon for soup. Your attempts at using chopsticks will be appreciated. When you are finished, set your chopsticks on the chopstick rest. Placing them parallel on top of your bowl is considered a sign of bad luck.
- Sticking your chopsticks straight up in your rice bowl is rude, as they will resemble the joss sticks used in religious ceremonies.
- Try not to drop your chopsticks; it is considered bad luck.
- Serving dishes are not passed around. Reach for food with your chopsticks, but do not use the end you put in your mouth! It is acceptable to reach in front of others to get to the serving dishes.
- Good topics of conversation include Chinese sights, art, calligraphy, and inquiries about the health of the other's family. Generally, conversation during a meal focuses on the meal itself and is full of compliments to the preparer.
- While the Chinese are not traditionally sports fans, their interest in sport has been increased by the Olympics. U.S. football is called "olive ball" in Mandarin Chinese because the ball is roughly olive-shaped.
- At a banquet, expect to be served rice in an individual bowl by a waiter. In a home, your hostess will serve the rice.

- Toasting is popular. At banquets, the host offers the first toast, and the ceremony continues all evening. It is acceptable to toast with a soft drink, but various alcoholic drinks will be available.
- Never take the last bit of food from a serving dish; this can signify that you are still hungry.
- The serving of fruit signals the end of the meal.
- If you do not want refills of tea, leave some in your cup.
- If you smoke, offer your cigarettes to others in your group. Many Chinese are heavy smokers.
- Historically, women did not drink alcoholic beverages. If the business dinner is extremely formal (like a black-tie event), businesswomen should accept a drink if offered, take a sip, and leave it. However, at a less formal affair (like a trade association dinner), women can now be the drinking representative!

Cultural Note
It is considered polite to sample every dish. The Chinese may even test your fortitude on purpose with exotic delicacies, like thousand-year-old eggs or marinated, deep-fried scorpions (completely intact with their stingers).

⊙ PROTOCOL

Greetings
- The Chinese nod or bow slightly when greeting another person, although handshakes are common. Wait for your Chinese associate to extend a hand first.
- Visitors to factories, theaters, or schools may be greeted with applause as a sign of welcome. The usual response is to applaud back.
- Introductions tend to be formal, with courtesy rather than familiarity preferred.

Titles/Forms of Address
- Names are listed in a different order from Western names. Each person receives a family name, a middle name (which used to be called a generational name), and a given name at birth—in that order.

Middle and given names can be separated by a space or a hyphen, but are often written as one word. For example, President Hu Jintao has the family name of Hu, a middle name of Jin, and a given name of Tao. (His name could also be rendered Hu Chin-t'ao.)

- The Chinese are very sensitive to status and titles, so you should use official titles such as "General," "Committee Member," or "Bureau Chief" when possible. Never call anyone "Comrade" unless you are a Communist also.
- Most people you meet should be addressed with a title and their name. If a person does not have a professional title (President, Engineer, Doctor), simply use "Mr." or "Madam," "Mrs.," or "Miss," plus the name.
- Chinese wives do not generally take their husband's surnames, but instead maintain their maiden names. Although Westerners commonly address a married woman as "Mrs." plus her husband's family name, it is more appropriate to call her "Madam" plus her maiden family name. For example, Liu Yongqing (female) is married to Hu Jintao (male). While Westerners would probably call her Mrs. Hu, she is properly addressed as Madam Liu.
- For more information on names and titles, see the section "Chinese Naming Conventions" in Appendix A.

Gestures
- Avoid making exaggerated gestures or using dramatic facial expressions. The Chinese do not use their hands when speaking, and become distracted by a speaker who does.
- The Chinese do not like to be touched by people they do not know. This is especially important to remember when dealing with older people or people in important positions.
- Members of the same sex may be seen publicly holding hands, but public affection between the opposite sexes is not condoned.
- Use an open hand rather than one finger to point.
- To beckon, turn the palm down and wave the fingers toward the body.
- Do not put your hands in your mouth (biting your nails, dislodging food from your teeth); this is considered disgusting.

Gifts

- Gift giving is a sensitive issue in China. While often in violation of Chinese law, gift giving is widespread.
- Avoid giving anything of value in front of others; it could cause the recipient both embarrassment and trouble.
- A gift from your company to the Chinese organization or factory is acceptable. Make it clear that the gift is on behalf of the whole company you represent and is for the whole group on the receiving end. Be sure to present the gift to the acknowledged leader of the Chinese delegation. Gifts of this sort might include items from your region of the country, like local crafts, historical memorabilia, or an illustrated book.
- A banquet is considered an acceptable gift. Your Chinese hosts will certainly give you one, and you should reciprocate.
- High-quality pens are appreciated. Other good gifts include gourmet food items and expensive liquors, like good cognac.
- Stamps are appreciate gifts if your associate is a collector (stamp collecting is popular in China). Cigarette lighters, T-shirts of well-known foreign sports teams, and electronic gadgets like iPods, electronic toys, etc. are also suitable. However, many of these items are made in China—be certain to make sure they are produced in your own home country!
- When giving or receiving a gift, use both hands. The gift is not opened in the presence of the giver.
- The Chinese traditionally decline a gift three times before accepting; this prevents them from appearing greedy. Continue to insist; once they accept the gift, say you are pleased that they have done so.
- Gifts of food are always appreciated by Chinese, but avoid bringing food gifts with you to a dinner or party (unless it has been agreed upon beforehand). To bring food may imply that your host cannot provide enough. Instead, send food as a thank-you gift afterward. Candy and fruit baskets are good choices.
- Older Chinese associate all of the following gifts and colors with funerals—avoid them:
  - Straw sandals
  - Clocks

- A stork or crane (although the Western association of storks with births is known to many young Chinese)
- Handkerchiefs (they symbolize sadness and weeping)
- Gifts (or wrapping paper) in which the predominant color is white, black, or blue.

- Do not wrap a gift before arriving in China; it may be unwrapped in Customs.
- If possible, wrap gifts in red, a lucky color. Pink and yellow are happy, prosperous colors, and are also good choices. Do not use white, which is the color for funerals. Ask about appropriate paper at your hotel or at a store that wraps gifts.
- All business negotiations should be concluded before gifts are exchanged.
- At Chinese New Year, it is customary to give a gift of money in a red envelope to children and to the service personnel that help you on a regular basis. This gift is called a *hong bao*. Give only new bills in even numbers and even amounts. Many employers give each employee a hong bao equivalent to one month's salary.

Dress

- For business, men should wear conservative suits, shirts, and ties. Loud colors are not appropriate. Women should also wear conservative suits, with relatively high-necked blouses and low heels—their colors should be as neutral as possible.
- At formal occasions, evening gowns are not necessary for women unless the event is a formal reception given by a foreign diplomat. Men may wear suits and ties.
- Casualwear is still somewhat conservative. Revealing clothing may be offensive, but jeans are acceptable for both men and women. Shorts are appropriate when exercising.

Cultural Note

Written Chinese does not have a future tense, or any other verb tense. Therefore, the sentence *"Wo mai shu"* can mean: I bought a book, I buy a book, or I will buy a book. Time frames can only be determined by the context of the sentence, or by time indicators like "tomorrow." Be very specific on times and dates for appointments, contracts, or other transactions.

Hong Kong

Hong Kong Special Administrative Region

> **Cultural Note**
>
> Hong Kong has always been a halfway point between China and the West. Today, it is the home of designers who are helping to brand China's manufactured products. China's emerging middle class wants prestigious names on their consumer goods, and Chinese manufacturers want to create an identity for themselves with Western consumers. Although a distinct Hong Kong style did not develop until the end of the twentieth century, Hong Kong designers are helping to brand products all over China.

▶ COUNTRY BACKGROUND

Demographics

Hong Kong packs 7 million inhabitants (2006 estimate) into its 1,092 square kilometers, giving it one of the highest population densities on the planet.

The Hong Kong Special Administrative Region includes Hong Kong Island, Kowloon, the New Territories, and numerous small islands.

History

Hong Kong's modern history begins with Imperial China's defeat in the First Opium War (1839–1842). Under the terms of the Treaty of Nanking, China was forced to cede Hong Kong Island to the United Kingdom. British and Scottish traders made Hong Kong their primary outpost for trade with China. The adjacent Kowloon Peninsula was added to Hong Kong after China's loss in the Second Opium War (1856–1858). The final expansion occurred in 1898, when the United Kingdom took a ninety-nine-year lease on what are called the

New Territories. Hong Kong remained a British colony for most of the twentieth century. British rule was interrupted only during the Second World War, when the Japanese occupied Hong Kong from 1941 to 1945.

After Mao Tse-tung's Communist forces took control of China in 1949, Hong Kong (along with Portugal's colony of Macao) became one of the only points of contact between China and the West. As the People's Republic of China consolidated its power, it became increasingly clear that the United Kingdom could not keep the People's Liberation Army from overrunning Hong Kong. After long negotiations, the United Kingdom agreed to give Hong Kong back to China. The People's Republic of China promised to respect the laws of Hong Kong, under a policy of "one country, two systems." The United Kingdom handed over its colony of Hong Kong to the People's Republic of China in 1997.

Type of Government

It is useful to remember that Hong Kong has never known self-rule. It was a colony of the United Kingdom from 1842 to 1997; only at the end of that period did the British allow the formation of a locally elected body, the Legislative Council (a.k.a., the Legco). The governor of Hong Kong was always appointed by London.

The former British colony is now the Hong Kong Special Administrative Region (SAR), part of the People's Republic of China, which has an authoritarian Communist government. To date, the chief executive of the Hong Kong SAR has been chosen by 800 electors, all of whom have been appointed by Beijing. The term of office of the chief executive is five years.

Current government data can be found at the Embassy of China at *www.china-embassy.org*.

Cultural Note

The British picked Hong Kong Island for its natural deep-water harbor—not for its weather. Hong Kong has a tropical monsoon climate. The best time to visit is during the fall, when it is warm and sunny. It is cool and humid in the winter. Spring and summer are hot and rainy.

Language

The Cantonese form of Chinese and English are the official languages. Since the takeover of Hong Kong by the PRC, more students
are studying Mandarin, which is the official language of China. Many
businesspeople speak English.

For data on the various languages of China, see the Ethnologue at
www.ethnologue.com.

The Hong Kong View

The British established the colony as a place to earn money, not
as a way to bring Western education, technology, or forms of government to the Chinese. And, although the Chinese of Hong Kong were
eventually exposed to all of these, they saw Hong Kong primarily as
a means to build wealth.

Hong Kong was also a place of refuge during unsettled times in
China, especially during the Communist takeover in 1949. Since
then, the PRC has closely guarded its border with Hong Kong. Even
today, Beijing determines how many "mainland" Chinese may visit
Hong Kong. (When China wants to boost the Hong Kong economy,
it allows many visitors to come and spend money.)

Hong Kong has often felt like a transitory home. Of course, many
businesspeople from the West are posted in Hong Kong for just a few
years. But Hong Kong has sometimes felt temporary to its Chinese
residents as well. Before the 1997 handover to China, many residents
of Hong Kong sought citizenship in other countries so that they
could flee if Beijing's rule became oppressive. Hong Kong's Chinese
were angered that the United Kingdom offered passports to relatively
few ethnic Chinese (but gave one to virtually all persons of British
descent). A substantial number of Hong Kong's wealthier citizens
immigrated to Canada.

Hong Kong has its own mini-constitution, known as its Basic Law.
According to the Sino-British Joint Declaration (1984) and the Basic
Law, Hong Kong will retain its political, economic, and judicial sys-
tems for fifty years following the 1997 handover. Furthermore, Hong
Kong will continue to participate in international agreements and
organizations under the name "Hong Kong, China." Consequently,

Hong Kong will keep its own special identity—at least for the next four decades.

Less than 45 percent of Hong Kong citizens participate in some form of religious practice. Of those who do, about 8 percent consider themselves Christians. Most religions are represented in Hong Kong; the city even has four Islamic mosques. However, Confucianism (a philosophy rather than a religion) dominates the culture.

As a trading center, the citizens of Hong Kong have learned to do business with partners from many countries. Perhaps the only country with which they have a problematic relationship is Japan. During the Second World War, Japan occupied Hong Kong on Christmas Day, 1941. The occupation was harsh: Many residents were executed, while others were exiled or interred. Thousands of women were raped. Food was confiscated for Japanese troops, leaving Hong Kong's remaining population to starve. By the end of the war, Hong Kong's population was down by about 1 million people.

There have been occasional anti-Japanese protests in Hong Kong, including one in April of 2005. However, little is taught about the Japanese occupation in Hong Kong schools. If the younger generations have negative viewpoints about the Japanese, it is primarily traced to Beijing's general opposition to Japan.

Cultural Note

Many residents of Hong Kong are sports fans. Horseracing is a popular spectator sport. The first horse race was run back in 1846, and the races have been part of Hong Kong life since then. The season runs from September through June, with races held on Wednesday evening and either Saturday or Sunday. Hong Kong has two racetracks, at Sha Tin and Happy Valley.

☑ Know Before You Go

Hong Kong has been a safe destination, except during periodic outbreaks of disease. New strains of influenza (while later spread worldwide) have often first been identified in Hong Kong. The most serious disease outbreak in recent times was that of SARS (severe acute respiratory syndrome), which killed almost 300 people in Hong Kong in 2003.

The residents of Hong Kong pride themselves on their legal system and their free flow of information; in this, they are much freer than their fellow citizens of the People's

Republic of China. But Beijing has not given up trying to bring Hong Kong into line. Beijing tried to impose an antisedition statute called Article 23 on Hong Kong in 2003. This would have reduced the city's freedoms, and Hong Kong residents responded with massive protests, forcing an indefinite postponing of the adoption of Article 23.

⊙ BUSINESS PRACTICES

Punctuality, Appointments, and Local Time

- The official format for writing dates in Hong Kong follows British tradition: day, month, and year. In this format, December 3, 2010, would be written 03/12/10, or 3.12.10. However, because influence is strong from the USA, some people use the U.S. pattern of month, day, and year. This renders December 3, 2010, as 12/3/10. To make matters even more confusing, the standard in the PRC is year/month/date. In this format, December 3, 2010, is written as 10/12/3. Naturally, if you have any question about a date, ask.

- Hong Kong, like China, is eight hours ahead of Greenwich Mean Time (G.M.T. + 8), or thirteen hours ahead of U.S. Eastern Standard Time (E.S.T. + 13).

Cultural Note

Chinese names can be rendered different ways in English, so do not be surprised by variations. Chinese normally have three names, and the most common variant is whether or not to hyphenate the final two names.

For example, the first chief executive of Hong Kong was Tung Chee Hwa. His name can also be rendered Tung Chee-hwa, or even Tung Cheehwa. (As with most Chinese, his surname is listed first, so he would be referred to as "Mr. Tung.")

Dress

- Hong Kong residents consider themselves better dressed and more fashionable than most Chinese. While this may be true for much of China, there are residents of Shanghai and Beijing who are equally stylish.

India

Republic of India

Cultural Note

India's government is determined to achieve self-sufficiency, and for decades has declined offers of outside help. In fact, after the tragic Boxing Day tsunami of 2004, not only did India decline outside aid, it provided assistance to its neighbors.

Indians tend to be very patriotic, and most support their government's efforts to increase their country's prestige. They believe that India should take its rightful place as one of the world's leading nations and as the leading military power in South Asia.

▶ WHAT'S YOUR CULTURAL IQ?

1. In 2004, a new prime minister of India was sworn in. TRUE or FALSE: He was the first Sikh to hold this position.
   ANSWER: TRUE. Prime Minister Manmohan Singh was a former International Monetary Fund official and finance minister. His priorities included better relations with Pakistan.

2. Many countries have decided to eradicate "colonial" or westernized versions of their cities' names. This movement began in western India in the 1990s and resulted in many changes all across India. Match the current city title with its former name.
   a. Mumbai   1. Calcutta
   b. Chennai   2. Bombay
   c. Kolkata   3. Madras
   ANSWER: a. 2; b. 3; c. 1

3. "Civilization is the encouragement of differences" is a quote by:
   a. Jawaharlal Nehru
   b. George W. Bush
   c. Mahatma Gandhi
   ANSWER: c. Mahatma Gandhi's dreams for a peaceful India have been buffeted by harsh realities in recent history, but his views are available online. One site is *www.mahatma.org.in*.

▶ TIPS ON DOING BUSINESS IN INDIA

- The workplace in India has changed drastically in the last few decades—from high-tech booms to Bollywood—the pace of decision making has sped up in many industry segments. However, traditional elements of doing business essentially remain the same. Networking, face-to-face meetings, and building relationships are still the means to success in India.

- Because some institutions have kept the old city names (for example, the Bombay Stock Exchange, the University of Madras, etc.) executives may keep two versions of their business cards. The one with the newer city names are for governmental officials, and the others are for international meetings with specific companies.

- Be aware that inadvertently supporting India's colonial past can generate serious repercussions with nationals. That past includes Portuguese and French terminology as well as English. Use one of India's 15 official languages for your advertisements and marketing materials whenever possible, and customize your products for Indian consumers. Also, be sure to contract with local agencies to verify that the subtleties of your promotional materials are not offensive.

- Highly educated Indians enjoy heated debates and feel strongly about defending their country's viewpoints. Keep an open mind, and never criticize India's poverty, belief systems, politics, caste system, or any business practices you may not understand or appreciate.

- Bargaining and negotiating is a continual lifestyle in India. Be prepared for multiple contract iterations.

▶ COUNTRY BACKGROUND

Demographics

India celebrated the birth of its billionth citizen in May of 2000. By 2006 the population figure was estimated at 1.1 billion, which encompasses dozens of different cultures, hundreds of holidays, languages, and belief systems. Its population is exceeded only by China.

History

The Indian subcontinent was home to advanced civilizations since before recorded history. It has also known its share of invaders. The Aryans (predecessors of the Hindus) conquered most of the subcontinent before 1500 B.C. The Muslim Moghuls ruled much of India until the advent of the European invaders. The Portuguese first arrived in 1489. French, Dutch, and English traders followed. The British East India Company became ascendant, essentially ruling India from 1760 to 1858, when India was formally transferred to the British Crown.

After long years of struggle and nonviolent resistance to British colonialism under Mohandas Gandhi and Jawaharlal Nehru, India became an independent country on August 15, 1947.

When the British left in 1947, British India was partitioned into primarily Hindu India and mostly Muslim Pakistan. The centuries-old antagonism between Hindus and Muslims has repeatedly erupted into open warfare between India and Pakistan since independence.

Type of Government

The Republic of India is a multiparty federal republic. The head of government is the prime minister, while the president is the chief of state. There are two multiparty legislative houses: the Council of States and the House of the People.

In the 1920s, Mahatma Gandhi made the Indian National Congress into India's leading political force. Its successor, the Congress Party, has ruled India for most of the years since independence.

India's first prime minister was Mahatma Gandhi's compatriot Jawaharlal Nehru. Power remained with the Congress Party until 1977, when Prime Minister Indira Gandhi (Nehru's daughter) was voted out of office. Janata Party leader Morarji Desai became prime minister, but his Janata coalition broke up in 1979. An interim government called new elections, and Indira Gandhi returned to power in 1980. She was assassinated by her own Sikh bodyguards in 1984, and she was succeeded by her son, Rajiv Gandhi. He attempted to steer the country toward a more market-oriented economy, but was defeated in the 1989 elections by another Janata coalition, and Vishwanath Pratap Singh became prime minister.

V. P. Singh's minority government's most serious crisis resulted from its determination to reserve some 49 percent of government jobs for lower castes (which make up 54 percent of India's 890 million people). Insurgencies in Punjab, Kashmi, and Assam further weakened the government. The Singh government fell in November 1990.

Rajiv Ghandi was assassinated during the elections of May 1991. In 1998 the Hindu nationalist BJP party formed a coalition under Prime Minister Atal Behari Vajpayee, and India performed their first nuclear tests. President Abdul Kalam, the former architect of India's missile program, was elected in 2002, and Manmohan Singh was sworn in as prime minister in a surprise victory for the Congress Party in 2004.

For current government data, visit the Embassy of India *www.indianembassy.org.*

Cultural Note

On March 12, 1930, Mahatma Gandhi began a 240-mile march, on foot, from Sabarmati to the coastal village of Dandi, in order to gather salt from the sea. The Salt March was in direct violation of British law, because the sale or production of salt by anyone but the British government was a criminal offense. However, up to one-fifth of a peasant's annual income could be consumed by the tax because salt was critical to the vegetarian diet of many Indians (particularly in India's intensely hot and humid climate). The twenty-three-day Salt March ultimately proved to be one of the major steps in India's fight for independence.

Language

Hindi is the national language, and English is an associate official language (widely used for business and political communications), but there are 14 other official languages and almost 400 others acknowledged by linguists. The 14 additional official languages are:

Assamese, Bengali, Gujarati, Kannada, Kashmiri, Malayalam, Marathi, Oriya, Panjabi, Sanskrit, Sindhi, Tamil, Telugu, and Urdu. Hindustani is a popular variant of Hindi/Urdu which is spoken widely throughout northern India but it is not an official language. The literacy rate is listed at approximately 60 percent.

More information on the languages of India can be found at *www .ethnologue.com*.

The Indian View

Religion plays a major role in the daily lives of most Indians, and two of the world's great religions—Buddhism and Hinduism—were born here.

The majority of Indians are Hindu. Unlike many religions that are traced to a particular founder, Hinduism grew out of Indian mythology. Hinduism has many variants and lacks a single, authoritative text (like the Christian Bible or the Muslim Koran). It is a religion with multiple gods, and it teaches a belief in karma and reincarnation. To escape the cycles of reincarnation and achieve nirvana, one must stop committing both bad deeds and good deeds—a difficult process which requires virtual nonintervention with humanity. India's caste system is supported by most variants of Hinduism. Many Hindus venerate cows and neither eat beef nor wear leather. Many Hindus are vegetarians.

Interestingly, Hinduism is still an evolving, dynamic religion. In some Hindu variants, new gods continue to be added to the pantheon. Indian film stars sometimes find themselves added to the Hindu pantheon!

A minority of Indians are Muslim. Islam is a monotheistic religion with ties to both Judaism and Christianity. Shiite Muslims outnumber Sunni Muslims by about three to one in India. Surrender to the will of Allah is a central belief. Pork and alcohol are prohibited to observant Muslims. While the majority of Hindus and Muslims coexist peacefully in India, violence does sometimes break out. Hundreds of people in both religions have died in religious conflicts.

About 2 percent of Indians are Sikhs. Sikhism combines tenets of both Hinduism and Islam. Sikhs believe in reincarnation but do not recognize caste distinctions. Unlike Hindus, Sikhs reject nonintervention with the world as cowardly.

India also has Christians, Buddhists, Jains, and Zoroastrians. The Republic of India has no official religion.

The origins of the caste system are unclear, but it has existed in India for thousands of years. Even though the government has outlawed discrimination on the basis of caste, castes still play a significant role in the politics and business of the country. Although there are only four traditional castes, these are broken down into thousands of subcastes.

☑ Know Before You Go

India has suffered everything from cyclones (in 1999 at least 10,000 died in the eastern state of Orissa) to massive earthquakes (approximately 30,000 dead in Gujarat during 2001) to the devastation of the tsunami in southern India in 2004. Additional hazards include droughts, flash floods from monsoons, and extreme weather changes in the Himalayas.

Stay healthy on your trip. Listen to your doctor's advice prior to your visit (and take your vaccinations against hepatitis A, cholera, etc.). Many travelers fall ill because of overindulging in spicy foods or eating raw fruits or vegetables that have been contaminated. Drink bottled water, wear sunscreen, and be certain to bring any required medications with you.

⦿ CULTURAL ORIENTATION

Cognitive Styles: How Indians Organize and Process Information

In India information is accepted openly as long as it does not challenge religious and social structures. Because of rote learning and tradition, most thinking is associative. However, highly educated Indians are more abstractive and analytical. Although universal rules of behavior exist within the social structure, immediate situations and people are of major concern, but always within the constructs of the caste system.

Negotiation Strategies: What Indians Accept as Evidence

Personal feelings form the basis for the truth, but a strong faith in religious ideologies is always present. The use of objective facts is less persuasive than a combination of feelings and faith.

Value Systems: The Basis for Behavior

Although it is constantly being challenged by younger citizens, India still has an attachment to the caste system, with all of its social structure and liabilities. The following three sections identify the Value Systems in the predominant culture—their mode of dividing right from wrong, good from evil, and so forth.

Locus of Decision-Making

India is a moderately collectivistic culture in which an individual's decisions must be in harmony with the family, group, and social structure. Success and failure are often attributed to environmental factors. Friendships and kinships are more important than expertise, although diplomas and certificates are coveted. One must build a relationship with other participants in the negotiation process by discussing friends and family. Indians may often be too polite to say "no."

Sources of Anxiety Reduction

With such a strong social structure, there is little anxiety about life because individuals know and accept their place in the society or organization. Behaviors contrary to religious traditions are not easily tolerated. There is a strong sense of what Westerners call "fatalism," so time is not a major source of anxiety, and passivity is a virtue. Emotions can be shown, and assertiveness is expected.

Issues of Equality/Inequality

There is a very rigid structure of inequality, even though there is equality under the law (seldom enforced). The belief that there are qualitative differences between the castes is ingrained. Traditional male chauvinism is strong, and women do not have equal privileges. The abundant sexual symbols in society do not translate into an acceptance of public intimacy.

Cultural Note

Tipping in India is more than just a reward for good service; it is often the way to ensure that things get done. The term *baksheesh* encompasses both these meanings. Judicious (and discreet) use of baksheesh will often open closed doors, such as getting a seat on a "sold-out" train.

▶ BUSINESS PRACTICES

Punctuality, Appointments, and Local Time

- Business hours vary all over India, but generally they are from 9:30 A.M. to 5:00 P.M., Monday through Friday (lunch is usually from 1:00 to 2:00 P.M.). Government office hours may be shorter, but they are open on some Saturdays.
- Indians appreciate punctuality but do not always practice it themselves. Keep your schedule loose enough for last-minute rescheduling of meetings.
- Request appointments as far ahead as possible. Advances in communication systems have made it far easier to schedule meetings, but it is still appropriate to get on the schedule of executives as early as possible.
- Be aware that your Indian contacts may request impromptu meetings at late hours.
- Make sure that you are fully equipped with the latest wireless and telecom devices before you arrive in India—your prospects will want multiple ways to contact you and will expect you to invest in technology.
- Although they usually do not make final decisions, middle managers do have input. A middle manager on your side can forward your proposal. Often they are more accessible, and they are willing to meet at any time of the day.
- Go to the top of the company for major decisions.
- Indian executives generally prefer late morning or early afternoon appointments, between 11:00 A.M. and 4:00 P.M.
- The best time of year to visit India is between October and March, bypassing the seasons of extreme heat and monsoons.

- Business is not conducted during religious holidays, which are numerous. Dates for these holidays change from year to year, so confirm your schedule with local contacts, and check for current holidays at *www.kissboworshakehands.com*.
- India is five and a half hours ahead of Greenwich Mean Time (G.M.T. + 5½), or ten and a half hours ahead of Eastern Standard Time (E.S.T. + 10½ hours).
- India operates in one time zone, and although it does not observe daylight-saving time, many visitors have mentioned their use of IST (Indian Stretchable Time).

Negotiating
- Indians have a less hurried attitude toward time than North Americans. The concept "time is money" is alien to many Indians.
- While you should get sound legal and tax advice before negotiating any agreement, it is important to be flexible and not appear too legalistic during negotiations.
- Be prepared to offer competitive technology packages with close technical follow-up. The technical assistance you can provide and how effective your training support is will be critical factors in the decision.
- Expect delays; they are inevitable. The Indian government moves at its own pace, and communication within India may still be somewhat difficult. Be patient, and make a realistic assessment of the steps and time involved in finalizing any agreements.
- Always present your business card. It is not necessary to have it translated into an Indian language.
- Business in India is highly personal. A great amount of hospitality is associated with doing business. Tea and small talk are preludes to most discussions.
- When refreshments are offered, it is customary to refuse the first offer, but to accept the second or third. To completely refuse any refreshment is an insult. Drink slowly if you wish to limit your intake of the sugary, milky Indian tea.
- The word "no" has harsh implications in India. Evasive refusals are more common, and are considered more polite. Never directly

refuse an invitation—just be vague and avoid a time commitment. "I'll try" is an acceptable refusal.

Cultural Note

In a monetary transaction, your change is simply placed in your hand, without explanation of the amount. If you remain standing with your hand outstretched, you may receive more change.

Be sure to keep lots of small change on hand, because street merchants and taxi drivers often claim they do not have change.

⊚ BUSINESS ENTERTAINING

- Business lunches are preferred to dinners.
- Remember that Hindus do not eat beef and Muslims do not eat pork.
- Businesswomen may host Indian businessmen at a meal without embarrassing the men, although the men may try to pay at the end of the meal. Female executives should arrange with the waiter to pay the bill before the meal.
- If you are invited to dinner, be a few minutes late unless it is an official function. If the dinner is in a home, you may arrive fifteen to thirty minutes late.
- Eat only with the right hand, because the left hand was traditionally used for hygienic purposes and is considered unclean.
- Touching a communal dish with your hands may cause fellow diners to avoid it.
- Never offer another person (even a spouse) food from your plate, as it is considered "polluted" as soon as it is placed on your plate.
- Washing your hands both before and after a meal is important. In Hindu homes, you are expected to rinse your mouth out as well.
- Do not thank your hosts at the end of a meal. Saying "thank you" for a meal is insulting because the thanks are considered a form of payment. Returning the meal by inviting your hosts to dinner shows that you value the relationship.
- India's two major religions abjure beef and pork, so it is not surprising that Indian cuisine uses mostly chicken, lamb, or vegetables.

Cultural Note

Here's one rude move you should be especially aware of in India. If you must share a bottle of water, tilt your head back and pour it into your mouth from above . . . without touching your lips. Don't put your mouth on the bottle and then try to pass it to the next parched soul. That would be *jootha*. The term "jootha" refers to a breach of conduct where your germs are being spread around, rather than your goodwill. Sharing is not always a virtue!

▶ PROTOCOL

Greetings

- In large cities, men and very westernized Indian women will offer to shake hands with foreign men and sometimes with foreign women. Western women should not initiate handshaking with Indian men.
- There are numerous ethnic, linguistic, and religious groups in India, each with its own traditions.
- The majority of Indians are Hindu. Most Hindus avoid public contact between men and women. Men may shake hands with men, and women with women, but only westernized Hindus will shake hands with the opposite sex.
- A minority of Indians are Muslim. Traditionally, there is no physical contact between Muslim men and women. Indeed, if an orthodox Muslim male is touched by a woman, he must ritually cleanse himself before he prays again. Because of this, women should not offer to shake hands with Muslim men (nor should men offer to shake hands with Muslim women). Of course, if a westernized Indian offers to shake hands, do so. Other Indian religious groups, such as Sikhs, also avoid public contact between the sexes.
- The traditional Indian greeting is the *namaste*. To perform the namaste, press the palms of your hands together (as if praying) below the chin, near the heart, and gently nod or bow slightly. There are many Web sites that describe the meaning of the namaste, and how this peaceful greeting can be appropriate for individuals or for large meetings.

- A namaste is useful for foreigners in any situation where a hand-shake might not be acceptable. It is also a good alternative to a handshake when a Western businesswoman greets an Indian man.
- Indians of all ethnic groups disapprove of public displays of affection between people of the opposite sex. Do not touch (except in handshaking), hug, or kiss in greeting.

Cultural Note

Giving money to a beggar will result in your being besieged by dozens of them. Unless you wish to distribute alms to many of India's poor, avoid even making eye contact.

When walking past an Indian temple, keep your hands in your pockets. If your hand is free, a stranger may offer to shake your hand. They are often street merchants who quickly slap a temple bracelet on your outstretched arm. Then you are expected to pay for the bracelet.

Titles/Forms of Address

- It is important to note that India's naming conventions are changing. For example, the Southern region of India seems to be gradually moving toward the naming customs of the North, and professional females are starting to keep their maiden names.
- Titles are highly valued by Indians. Always use professional titles, such as "Professor" and "Doctor." Don't address someone by his or her first name unless you are asked to or you are close friends; use "Mr.," "Mrs.," or "Miss."
- For a full discussion of titles and forms of address in India, see Appendix A.

Cultural Note

Among Indians, a side-to-side toss of the head indicates agreement, although Westerners may interpret it as meaning "no." Watch carefully; the Indian head toss is not quite the same as the Western negative nod (which leads with the jaw).

On the other hand, the North American up-and-down head nod (used to signify "yes") can be confusing to Indians, because a form of that gesture can imply "no" in India.

Gestures

- Many Indians consider the head to be the seat of the soul. Never touch someone else's head, not even to pat the hair of a child.
- As in much of the world, to beckon someone, you hold your hand out, palm downward, and make a scooping motion with the fingers. Beckoning someone with the palm up and wagging one finger can be construed as an insult.
- Standing tall with your hands on your hips—the "arms akimbo" position (also the gesture for "Offsides!" in soccer)—will be interpreted as an angry, aggressive posture.
- The comfortable standing distance between two people in India varies with the culture. In general, Hindu Indians tend to stand about three or three and a half feet apart.
- Pointing with a finger is rude; Indians point with the chin.
- Whistling under any circumstances is considered impolite.
- Winking may be misinterpreted as either an insult or a sexual proposition.
- Grasping your ears designates sincerity or repentance. Ears are considered sacred appendages; to pull or box someone's ears is a great insult.
- Never point your feet at a person. Feet are considered unclean. If your shoes or feet touch another person, apologize.

Gifts

- Gifts are not opened in the presence of the giver. If you receive a wrapped gift, set it aside until the giver leaves.
- If you are invited to an Indian's home for dinner, bring a small gift of chocolates or flowers. Don't give frangipani blossoms, however—they are associated with funerals.
- Don't wrap gifts in black or white, which are considered unlucky colors; green, red, and yellow are lucky colors.
- If you know that your Indian counterpart drinks alcohol, bring imported whiskey. High taxes can be avoided by purchasing the liquor on the airline or at the duty-free shop before arriving.
- Muslims consider dogs unclean. Do not give toy dogs or gifts with pictures of dogs to Indian Muslims.

- Should you give money to an Indian, make sure it is an odd number. Usually this is done by adding a single dollar; for example, give $11 instead of $10.
- For more guidelines on culturally correct gifts in India, visit *www .kissboworshakehands.com.*

Dress
- For business dress, men should wear a suit and tie, although the jacket may be removed in the summer. Businesswomen should wear conservative dresses or pantsuits.
- For casual wear, short-sleeved shirts and long trousers are preferred for men; shorts are acceptable only while jogging. Women must keep their upper arms, chest, back, and legs covered at all times. Women who jog should wear long pants.
- Note that wearing leather (including belts, handbags, or purses) may be considered offensive, especially in temples. Hindus revere cows, and do not use leather products.

Indonesia

Republic of Indonesia
Local long form: Republik Indonesia
Former: Netherlands East Indies; Dutch East Indies

Cultural Note

While the word for "tomorrow" in Bahasa Indonesian is *besok*, this word does not literally mean "within the next 24 hours." It can mean the day after, or the day after that, or it might even mean next week. Besok is like the Spanish *mañana* in that it denotes the near future.

▶ WHAT'S YOUR CULTURAL IQ?

1. Indonesia is an equatorial archipelago, marking the boundaries of the Indian and Pacific Oceans. TRUE or FALSE? Indonesia comprises at least 13,000 islands.
   ANSWER: TRUE. The exact number varies, according to one's definition of what constitutes an island. Some sources put the figure as high as 17,000.

2. Indonesia contains an astonishing diversity of wildlife, from giant lizards to orangutans. TRUE or FALSE: Zoologists say that Indonesia straddles what is known as the "Wallace Line."
   ANSWER: TRUE. The Wallace Line is the dividing point between Asian and Australian flora and fauna. Parts of Indonesia are on either side of this line.

3. Which of the following leaders is considered Indonesia's first freely elected head of state?
   a. Sukarno
   b. Suharto
   c. B. J. Habibie
   d. Megawati Sukarnoputri

ANSWER: d. Sukarno and Suharto seized power. B. J. Habibie was Suharto's vice president, and took over when protestors forced Suharto out in 1998. The country's first free election for president occurred in 1999, when the daughter of Sukarno, Megawati Sukarnoputri, was elected president.

▶ TIPS ON DOING BUSINESS IN INDONESIA

- Be punctual to all business appointments. As a foreign business-person, you are expected to be on time. However, it would be unrealistic to expect punctuality from all Indonesians, because promptness has not traditionally been considered a virtue. Furthermore, making people wait can be an expression of Indonesia's social structure. It is the prerogative of a person of higher standing to make a person of lower rank wait, and it is very poor manners for a person of lower rank to show anger or displeasure toward a person in a higher station.

- Even foreigners are expected to be late to social events. As a general rule, arrive about a half-hour late. But be aware that there is complex social interplay at social events. Some Indonesians will attempt to arrive later than lesser personages but earlier than more important guests. (For this reason, invitations to some events may state a time, but will add "please arrive fifteen minutes early." This is to ensure that no one arrives after the most important guest.)

- Indonesians show great deference to a superior. Consequently, supervisors are often told what they want to hear. The truth is conveyed in private, "up the grapevine"—often by a friend of the superior. Indonesians honor their boss by shielding him from bad news in public. This Indonesian trait, called *asal bapak senan'* (which translates as "keeping father happy") is instilled in Indonesians from childhood. A foreign executive must establish a network through which he or she can be told the truth in private.

- Because Indonesians believe it is impolite to openly disagree with someone, they rarely say "no." The listener is expected to be perceptive enough to discern a polite "yes (but I really mean no)" from an actual "yes." This is rarely a problem when speaking in Bahasa Indonesia, because the language has at least twelve ways to say "no" and many ways to say "I'm saying yes, but I mean no." This subtlety is lost when translated into many foreign languages, including English.

- Indonesians are comfortable with silence, in both business and social settings. A silent pause does not necessarily signal either acceptance or rejection. Westerners often find such pauses uncomfortable, but Indonesians do not "jump" on the end of someone else's sentence. A respectful pause may last as long as ten to fifteen seconds. Westerners often assume they have agreement and resume talking before an Indonesian has the chance to respond.

Cultural Note

As Indonesia is a relatively new nation, it is not surprising that it has a relatively short literary history. Indonesia has proven to be a fairly difficult place for journalists as well. Journalists who write things that displease the government have often been arrested (or, if foreigners, ordered to leave the country). Journalists found guilty of "criminal defamation" have been imprisoned (the editor of *Tempo* magazine, Bambang Harymurti, was sentenced to twelve months imprisonment in 2004).

▶ COUNTRY BACKGROUND

Demographics
As a geographically divided archipelago with many diverse ethnic and religious groups, Indonesia struggles to maintain unity among its 245 million inhabitants (2006 estimate). These ethnic groups include Javanese (45 percent of Indonesia's population), Sundanese (14 percent), Madurese, Chinese, Buginese, Batak, Dayak, Balinese, Minangkabau, and many others.

History
Thanks to its central location, Indonesia has been a trading outpost for many centuries. Chinese trading settlements in Indonesia were established as early as the third century B.C. However, it was Indian traders who eventually had the greatest influence upon early

Indonesia. By the second century A.D., several small states had organized on Indian models and flourished on Sumatra, Java, and Borneo.

Many Indian influences are to be seen in modern Indonesia.
Although Hinduism was superseded by Islam on most islands, it is
still the main religion on Bali. The native language of Java is written
in a variant of the Indian Devanagari alphabet.

Contact with Europe began in the sixteenth century. Beginning
in 1511, the Portuguese dominated the region from their base in
Malacca, in neighboring Malaysia. The Dutch arrived in 1596; they
eventually reduced the Portuguese holdings in Indonesia to the eastern half of the island of Timor. Indonesia was ruled by the Dutch East
India Company from 1602 to 1798, when the Dutch government took
direct control. Nationalist sentiments grew during the early twentieth
century, but Indonesia remained a Dutch colony until World War
II. The Japanese occupied Indonesia from 1942 to 1945. During this
occupation, native Indonesians were finally placed in positions of
power and allowed by the Japanese to run the nation. One such leader,
Sukarno, declared Indonesia an independent republic on August 17,
1945. The Dutch fought to regain control of Indonesia, but they finally
relinquished all claims to their former colony in 1949.

When the Western powers refused to support him against the
remaining Dutch presence in the area, Sukarno became hostile
toward the West and received military assistance first from the USSR,
then from the People's Republic of China. Most Indonesian political parties were restricted in order to allow the Communist Party of
Indonesia (PKI) to become the dominant political force.

With Sukarno in ill health, the PKI decided to take power in a coup
on September 30, 1965. The coup failed, and for the next six months
Indonesia writhed in civil disorder. In 1966, President Sukarno was
forced out of power and General Suharto became president.

Although Indonesia was officially a nonaligned nation, Suharto
pursued friendlier relations with the West. Since Suharto's accession
in 1966, Indonesia pursued a probusiness, proinvestment policy that
brought increased prosperity and development.

In May of 1998, the long-simmering political discontent with the
authoritarian rule of President Suharto erupted into violence. Under

pressure, President Suharto resigned, and Vice President B. J. Habibie took power. An election—the first free election in Indonesian history—was held in May 1999. Despite the advantages of money, experience, and control of the media, the long-ruling party of Habibie and Suharto failed to win a majority in the election.

After the people of the Indonesian state of East Timor voted for independence in August of 1999, the government in Jakarta allowed legions of Indonesian soldiers and militias to run riot in East Timor. Thousands of Timorese were slain, tens of thousands fled the country, and many homes and businesses were burned. The world was outraged, and Jakarta reluctantly agreed to allow UN troops into East Timor. Peace was eventually restored, and East Timor became an independent country on 20 May 2002.

Cultural Note

Since achieving independence after World War II, Indonesia went from a subsistence economy to becoming one of the "young dragons" of the Pacific Rim. Its abundant natural resources and a prodevelopment government made Indonesia a focus of foreign investment.

While Indonesia has suffered economic reverses, most economists assume that it has the population and the resources to resume its rapid growth—as long as it achieves political stability. However, some observers believe that separatist demands will force Indonesia to break up.

Type of Government

The Republic of Indonesia declared its independence in 1945. Fighting against the Dutch continued until 1949, which is the usual date given for Indonesian independence.

Indonesia is a unitary multiparty republic. The president is both head of state and head of the government. The Republic of Indonesia has two legislative houses, the House of People's Representatives and the People's Consultative Assembly.

As a diverse nation, separated by geography, language, ethnicity, and religion, Indonesia must constantly struggle against separatism and secession. Areas of Indonesia threatened by separatist movements are Aceh, Kalimantan, Sulawesi, the Molucca Islands, and

Papua (formerly known as Irian Jaya). After a referendum and international pressure, East Timor was granted independence in 2002.

For current government data, visit the Embassy of Indonesia at *www.embassyofindonesia.org.*

Cultural Note

The government has established an official doctrine called *Pancasila,* which affirms the existence of a single Supreme Being. This is in harmony with both Islam and Christianity, Indonesia's second largest religious grouping (9.6 percent of the population). It is, however, in opposition to Indonesia's minority Hindus (1.8 percent). The five principles of Pancasila are:

- Belief in One Supreme God.
- Belief in a just and civilized humanity.
- Belief in the unity of Indonesia.
- Belief in democracy.
- Belief that adherence to Pancasila will bring social justice to all of Indonesia.

All Indonesian government employees and all students are indoctrinated in Pancasila.

Language

The Republic of Indonesia has designated Bahasa Indonesia as the official language. Written in the Roman alphabet, Bahasa Indonesia evolved out of the "market Malay" trade language used throughout the region during the colonial era. The selection of Bahasa Indonesia as the official tongue was a conscious effort to unify all Indonesians; as a trade language, it did not have the literary history or prestige of other Indonesian tongues (notably Javanese). Bahasa Indonesia is written horizontally, left to right, using the Roman alphabet used in the West.

While as many as 140 million Indonesians use Bahasa Indonesia as a second language, no more than 30 million consider it their mother tongue. Almost half the population of Indonesia uses Javanese as its first language.

The Indonesian archipelago encompasses one of the most linguistically dense areas of the world. Ethnologue, at *www.ethnologue.com,* has identified 731 languages in Indonesia, 3 of which are extinct. All advertising, media, and official communications are required to be in Bahasa Indonesia, and it is taught in all elementary schools.

The Indonesian View

The early traders and settlers brought Hinduism and Buddhism to Indonesia (the Majapahit empire merged the two into a single state religion). Islam arrived in the sixteenth century and eventually became Indonesia's major religion. As with earlier religions, the Indonesians adapted Islam to suit their needs, especially on the island of Java. Indonesia, with its 245 million people, is the world's most populous Islamic nation. However, Islam in Indonesia is fragmented into numerous sects, many of which are antagonistic toward one another.

The majority of Indonesians are Muslim. While Islam is not the official religion, Indonesia has declared itself to be officially monotheistic. Of course, this position is in accordance with Islam and in opposition to Hinduism.

In addition to ethnic and religious factionalism, Indonesians must deal with economic problems, a developing democracy, and a history of corruption on the part of their leaders. Under Sukarno, Indonesia had a system of "crony capitalism," in which business licenses were dependent upon the favor of friends and family of Sukarno.

Indonesia's former colonial owner, the Netherlands, exerts relatively little influence over Indonesia today (although the Netherlands remains a highly desired destination for Indonesian emigrants). The USA is a major influence, although Indonesians have some justification for being angry at the USA in regard to East Timor (in 1976 the United States indicated that it did not object to Indonesia's annexation of East Timor, but by 1999 the USA started putting pressure on Indonesia to grant independence to East Timor). Since the terrorist attacks of 11 September 2001, Indonesian terrorists have become a large concern. However, when foreign troops are on Indonesian soil—as with the majority of the UN troops in East Timor—they are usually Australian. Until the recent bombings, Australians also made up the bulk of foreign tourists in Indonesia.

The new player in Indonesian affairs is the People's Republic of China, which is increasing its influence all over Asia. Because much of Indonesian business is in the hands of ethnic Chinese, the PRC has a built-in advantage. However, this advantage is tempered by the distrust that many ethnic Malays have for Indonesian Chinese. If there is another pogrom by Malays against Indonesian Chinese, the PRC may decide to act.

☑ Know Before You Go

Indonesia is well within the Pacific "Ring of Fire," and like many other countries, suffered horribly from the tsunamis generated by the earthquake of 2004.

There is no aspect of Indonesia that was not touched by the tsunami. While it is well nigh impossible to predict such a terrible event, travelers should take precautions when visiting any of the countries that were hit by the tragedy. Be certain to register with your country's embassy or consulate when you visit, and leave details of your trip with multiple contacts at home. Make it as easy as possible for people to track you down in an emergency. Indonesia is also subject to volcanic eruptions. Flooding and typhoons are a danger as well.

While Western foreigners—especially from the USA and Australia—have been targeted by bombings, the majority of visitors experience no hostility in Indonesia. However, check with your country's government as to whether or not there are any current travel advisories for Indonesia. Mob violence is probably more of a danger than the occasional terrorist acts.

Air quality is a sometimes a problem in Indonesian cities. Smoking is common and there are relatively few nonsmoking areas. During extended dry seasons, smoke from slash-and-burn agriculture has become so omnipresent that it sometimes darkens the sky and poses a threat to aviation.

Cultural Note

Life in Indonesia is made possible by a series of small bribes, known as *pungli* in Bahasa Indonesian. Such bribes may be needed for the simplest of transactions, from getting municipal services to facilitating transportation. If the recipient has to ask you for the payoff, the price automatically goes up. Indonesians look at pungli as Westerners look at tips, except that pungli are paid before the service is given rather than after.

▶ CULTURAL ORIENTATION

Cognitive Styles: How Indonesians Organize and Process Information

Indonesians have a history of assimilating new ways of doing things into their indigenous systems. They are open to information.

Independent thinking is discouraged in their education, so they tend to process information associatively. Those educated abroad may be more abstractive. Their focus is on the immediate situation and the people involved rather than on rules or laws that might govern behavior in similar situations.

Negotiation Strategies: What Indonesians Accept as Evidence

Most people will rely on the truth of their subjective feelings. However, this truth may be modified by a faith in the ideology of their religion. The most powerful influence is the desire for harmony. Those with higher education may accept objective facts more readily.

Value Systems: The Basis for Behavior

One should be aware of the value system of the Chinese, who conduct much of the business in Indonesia. Indonesians have blended Hinduism, Buddhism, Islam, and Christianity into their theology. The following three sections identify the Value Systems in the predominant culture—their methods of dividing right from wrong, good from evil, and so forth.

Locus of Decision-Making

Decision-making traditionally goes through deliberation and consensus. All interested parties are welcome to participate. They strive for balance; conciliation without resentments or grudges is a trait of the Indonesian culture. Many government officials and entrepreneurs adhere to a mystical form of spirituality called Kebatinan, a metaphysical search for inner harmony and guidance in decision-making. They do not subjugate the will of the individual to the will of the group.

Sources of Anxiety Reduction

There is a strong belief in the supernatural for protection and security. This faith goes beyond any one religion, although most Indonesians are at least nominally Muslims. The nuclear and extended families are basic to security and economic support, with marriage being used to reinforce economic and social alliances. The *adat* (common law) has become one of the major stabilizing factors maintaining the traditional rural societies. The military is the main arbiter of power in the government.

Issues of Equality/Inequality

In most organizations there is a strong authoritarian hierarchical system that demands obedience of subordinates. Although there are strong ethnic identities, there is also a strong national identity that is taught to all children in the primary school years. The husband is considered the head of the household, but the wife is not inferior in status, and both are expected to cooperate in maintaining their household and family. Equal rights for women have always been upheld in the community.

Nevertheless, Indonesia has a multiethnic society with many historic antagonisms. In particular, ethnic Chinese and Christian Indonesians are sometimes the targets of antagonism.

⊙ BUSINESS PRACTICES

Punctuality, Appointments, and Local Time

- Although the majority of Indonesians are Muslim, Indonesia does not follow the traditional Islamic work week pattern (Friday is the Islamic holy day, so the traditional Muslim "weekend" is Thursday and Friday). Instead, the work week runs four full days, Monday through Thursday, then two half days on Friday and Saturday.
- As a foreign businessperson, you are expected to be on time for all business appointments. This is especially true when you are meeting someone with a higher social standing than yourself.
- In general, the higher the status of an Indonesian, the more he or she is likely to appreciate punctuality. Sometimes Indonesian laborers consider themselves punctual if they arrive within a few hours of an appointment. Executives and government officials will understand promptness—but they still have the prerogative to make a subordinate wait.
- A majority of Indonesian businesspeople are Chinese. Their culture is very work oriented, and they are likely to be prompt.

Other businesspeople and the majority of government officials are ethnic Malays. Their culture is very different from that of the Chinese, and they have a looser concept of time. Promptness has never been a virtue in the Malay culture of Indonesia.

- Social events in Indonesia involve different rules. In general, Indonesians arrive a half-hour late.
- The casual Indonesian attitude toward time may allow you to schedule appointments on short notice.
- Indonesian executives tend to be more accessible than executives in many countries. Even an Indonesian CEO is likely to meet with foreign businesspeople.
- English is used in many business transactions and correspondence. However, attempts to use Bahasa Indonesia are appreciated.
- Bahasa Indonesia is the official language of Indonesia. Although many government officials will speak some English, they may prefer to hold meetings in their native tongue. Fortunately, an English-speaking translator is usually close at hand.
- All official correspondence with government officials must be in Bahasa Indonesia. Use of the language is also mandated for many advertisements and publications.
- The holidays in Indonesia attempt to accommodate the celebrations of Islam, Hinduism, and Christianity. For the official holidays of Indonesia, visit *www.kissboworshakehands.com.*
- Observant Muslims fast from dawn to sundown during the month of Ramadan. Be sure not to eat or drink in front of fasting Indonesians. It can be difficult to conduct business during Ramadan, when many Indonesians leave to visit relatives in rural areas—or even on another island. The price of food, clothing, and transportation tends to rise during Ramadan.
- As in most countries, Indonesians write the day first, then the month, and then the year (e.g., December 3, 2010, is written 3/12/10 or 3.12.10).
- Indonesia spans three time zones. Java and Bali are on West Indonesia Standard Time, which is seven hours ahead of Greenwich Mean Time (G.M.T. + 7). Central Indonesia Standard Time is eight hours ahead of Greenwich Mean Time (G.M.T. + 8); Lombok and

Nusatenggara are on Central Time. The East Indonesia Standard
Time Zone, which includes Maluku and Papua (Irian Jaya), is nine
hours ahead of Greenwich Mean Time (G.M.T. + 9).

Cultural Note

Expect to encounter tough negotiations. Indonesians negotiate virtually every aspect of their
daily lives, from taxi rides to groceries. You should anticipate considerable haggling over
even the smallest point. In addition, Indonesians are good at wearing down the opposition,
because the concept "time is money" is not a cultural norm.

Negotiating

- Indonesians do business with people they know and like. Establishing this personal relationship will take time, but it is vital for
  success.
- The pace of business negotiations in Indonesia is far slower than
  in the West. Be patient and do not rush.
- It would be unusual to complete a complicated business deal in
  only one trip. Expect to take several trips over a period of months.
  Indeed, little will happen at the first meeting except getting
  acquainted.
- Politeness is one of the most important attributes for successful
  relationships in Indonesia. This politeness in no way hinders the
  determination of Indonesian businesspeople to get their own way.
- Everyone has a defined status in Indonesia. In Bahasa Indonesia,
  you generally converse with a person after you know whether he
  or she is your superior, inferior, or equal. Even when the conversation is in English, Indonesians will not feel comfortable until
  they know your position. This is one reason why Indonesians will
  ask you very personal questions about your job, your education,
  and your salary.
- Indonesians rarely say "no" because they consider it impolite to
  disagree with someone. You are expected to be perceptive enough
  to differentiate a polite "yes (but I really mean no)" from an
  actual "yes." This is rarely a problem when speaking in Bahasa

Indonesia, because the language has at least twelve ways to say "no" and many ways to say, "I'm saying 'yes' but I mean no." This subtlety is lost in English. Westerners sometimes interpret this as deceit, but Indonesians are simply being polite by their own cultural standards.

- This "no" is clear even in English: anytime an Indonesian says "yes, but . . . ," it means "no."
- When there are any qualifications attached (such as, "It might be difficult"), it means "no."
- A clear way to indicate "no" is to suck in air through the teeth. This sound always indicates a problem.
- Evasion is indicative of a "no," even if the person has said neither "yes" nor "no." He or she may even pretend the question was never asked.

- A deal is never complete until all the paperwork is signed. Indonesians (especially the Chinese) often consult astrologers, so the signing may be delayed until an "auspicious" day arrives.
- People in Indonesia may smile or laugh in situations that Westerners consider inappropriate. Smiles may hide embarrassment, shyness, bitterness, or discord. If an Indonesian nurse giggles while tending to a seriously ill male patient; this could be from embarrassment at having to touch a man, not callousness. Learning to interpret smiles and laughter may take a foreigner years.
- In Indonesia, an individual who expresses anger in public is considered unable to control himself or herself. Such a person will not be trusted or respected.
- Being embarrassed publicly (also called "losing face") is known as *malu*. One result of "malu mentality" is that Indonesians may allow a person to continue to err rather than risk embarrassment by correcting him or her in public. In effect, an Indonesian may "honor" someone's authority by allowing him or her to make a disastrous error.
- It is considered polite among Indonesian Chinese to offer both the positive and negative options in virtually every decision. Even when speaking in English, they are likely to add a "yes/no" pattern

to a question. Rather than asking, "Would you like to have dinner?" they are likely to ask, "You want dinner or not?" The phrases involved ("want or not want," "good or not," "can or cannot") are direct translations of Chinese phrases into English. They may sound unduly aggressive to Western ears.

Cultural Note

The Indonesian term *jam karet* (rubber time) refers to the indigenous casual attitude toward time. Only a true emergency, such as a death or serious illness, will impel many ethnic Indonesians to make haste.

- Be cautious in asking an Indonesian Chinese a question. English speakers would give a negative answer to the question "Isn't my order ready yet?" by responding, "no" (meaning, "no, it's not ready"). The Chinese pattern is the opposite: "yes" (meaning, "yes, it is not ready").
- Indonesians of all ethnic groups are comfortable with silence, in both business and social settings. A silent pause allows time for thought; it does not necessarily signal either acceptance or rejection. Westerners often find such pauses uncomfortable.
- In Indonesia, individuals are rarely singled out in public, either for praise or for condemnation. People are expected to be part of a group, and it is the group that is addressed. If you must reprimand an individual employee, do it calmly and in private.
- Always be aware of social hierarchy. If you are part of a delegation, line up so that the most important persons will be introduced first. If you are introducing two people, state the name of the most important person first (e.g., "President Suhardjono, this is Engineer Wong").
- Speak in quiet, gentle tones. Always remain calm. Leave plenty of time for someone to respond to a statement you make (as long as ten to fifteen seconds) before speaking again. Westerners often assume that they have agreement and resume talking before a Indonesian has the chance to respond.
- Topics to avoid in conversation include any criticism of Indonesian ways, religion, bureaucracy, human rights record, or politics.

Also, avoid any discussion of sex or the roles of the sexes. (However, do not be surprised to hear graphic discussions of birth control methods. The Indonesian government supports major population control programs.)

- Good topics for discussion include tourism, travel, plans for the future, organizational success (talking about personal success is considered impolite boasting), and food (while remaining complimentary to the local cuisine). Stories about your attempts to learn Bahasa Indonesia also make good conversation.

Business Entertaining

- Some Indonesians have negative images of foreigners. Indonesia was exploited by foreigners for some 300 years. Social encounters are the best way for you to dispel that preconceived image.
- Understand that there may be little conversation while eating. Do not be concerned by a silent meal.
- Take advantage of any invitations to social events. Establishing a successful business relationship hinges on establishing a social relationship as well.
- Invitations to social events may not come immediately. Be patient and let your Indonesian associates make the first invitation. You generally do not host a social event until you have already been a guest.
- Respond to written invitations in writing. Among the Chinese, white and blue are colors associated with sadness; do not print invitations with those colors. Red or pink is a good choice.
- Generally, spouses may be invited to dinner but not to lunch. However, no business will be discussed at an event where spouses are present.

⊚ PROTOCOL

Greetings

- Indonesia has more than 300 ethnic groups, each with its own traditions. These range from isolated Stone Age tribes in the jungles of Irian Jaya to the cosmopolitan denizens of Jakarta.

- Expect to shake hands only upon initial introductions and before and after a long separation. Most Indonesian handshakes are more like handclasps; they are rather gentle and last for some ten or twelve seconds. (By contrast, most North American handshakes last for only three or four seconds.) For special emphasis, the handshake can be intensified by placing your hand over your heart.

Cultural Note

Hosting a party for Indonesians can be complex. Send out written invitations (addressed to husband and wife) a week in advance, but do not expect many responses in writing, even if your invitations say RSVP. Indonesians are somewhat averse to committing themselves to a social event. Find excuses to follow up (either by phone or in person) to remind your guests of the affair. Be prepared to explain (1) what event the party is celebrating, (2) the guest list, and (3) who the guest of honor is. Hold the party early; the guests will probably leave by 9:30 P.M. Indonesians find buffets more comfortable than sit-down dinners with assigned places. Be sure the food is sophisticated; if you depend on Indonesian servants to plan the meal, they are likely to select working-class fare (tasty but not prestigious). Remember that observant Muslims do not drink alcohol. Finally, show great respect toward your guest of honor. He (or she) is the last to arrive and the first to be served.

- Most ethnic Indonesians are Muslim; the majority of the others are Hindu. Traditionally, there is no physical contact between men and women in these cultures. (Indeed, if a religious Muslim male is touched by a woman, he must ritually cleanse himself before he prays again.) Because of this, women should not offer to shake hands with Indonesian men (nor should men offer to shake hands with Indonesian women). Of course, if a westernized Indonesian offers to shake hands, do so.
- Upon greeting, the traditional Muslim Indonesian salutation is the word *selamat*, which means "peace."
- Among Indonesian Chinese, the traditional greeting was a bow. However, most now shake hands or combine a bow with a handshake. Chinese men are more likely than other Indonesian ethnic groups to be comfortable shaking hands with a woman.
- The traditional Hindu greeting involves a slight bow with the palms of the hands together (as if praying). This greeting, called

the namaste, will generally be used only by older, traditional Hindus. However, it is also an acceptable alternative to a handshake when a Western businesswoman greets a Hindu Indonesian man.

- Above all else, greetings in Indonesia are stately and formal. Do not rush. Take your time; hurried introductions show a lack of respect. This applies to all Indonesians, from executives to laborers.

- Among all ethnic groups, kissing in public (even a quick peck on a cheek) is considered unacceptable. Only the most fashionable and cosmopolitan of Indonesians will give even a quick kiss in greeting.

Cultural Note

Just as the British greeting "How do you do?" is rhetorical, Indonesians have many rhetorical greetings. Chinese greetings often involve food. "Have you eaten?" and "Have you taken food?" are rhetorical greetings; answer "Yes," even if you are hungry. Similarly, a typical Indonesian greeting when meeting on the street is "Where are you going?" This is also rhetorical; "For a walk" or "Nowhere of importance" is a perfectly acceptable answer ("I'm eating the wind!" is a local idiomatic response). You are not expected to reveal your itinerary.

- Business cards should be printed (preferably embossed) in English. Since ethnic Chinese constitute the majority of Indonesian businesspeople, you may wish to have the reverse side of some of your cards printed in Chinese (gold ink is the most prestigious for Chinese characters).

- Your business card should contain as much information as possible, including your business title and your qualifications. Indonesians include all of this data on their card, as well as any titles of nobility.

- Westerners should use their usual academic titles, rather than translate them into the Indonesian equivalent (which are sometimes derived from Dutch academic titles).

- The exchange of business cards can be quite stately. After introductions are made, the visiting businessperson should offer his or her card to each person present. Present your card with both hands. (The most deferential method is to present your card in your right hand, with your left hand lightly supporting your right wrist.) Give your card to the recipient with the print facing him or her (so he or she can read it). The recipient will receive the card with both hands, then study the card for a few moments before carefully putting it away in a pocket. You should do the same when a card is presented to you.

- Never put a business card in your back pocket, where many men carry their wallets. While it is useful to write information such as the pronunciation of a name on someone's business card, do not let the person see you writing on his or her card. Either of these actions may be interpreted as "defiling" a business card.

Titles/Forms of Address

- Every variation of personal naming patterns can be found among Indonesia's myriad ethnic groups. People may have one name or two, short names or long, given name followed by a family name or vice versa, or one name and one initial.

- Names are considered sacred by most Indonesians. Indeed, among some Javanese, a person who has a string of misfortunes will change his or her name to one considered luckier.

- Most businesspeople you meet should be addressed with at least a title and their name. If a person does not have a professional title (such as Engineer, Doctor, or Teacher), a Westerner may use "Mr." or "Madam," "Mrs.," or "Miss," plus their name. However, be aware that you may be omitting other titles, important both to the person and your understanding of that person.

- As you inquire of an Indonesian how you should address him or her, be forward in explaining what he or she should call you. Indonesians may be equally unsure as to which of your names is your surname. Follow their lead as to the degree of formality. Do not tell an Indonesian "just call me Tony" when you are calling him Dr. Armizal.

- For more information on Chinese and Muslim naming conventions, see Appendix A.

Gestures

- Aside from handshakes, there is no public contact between the sexes in Indonesia. Do not kiss or hug a person of the opposite sex in public—even if you are husband and wife. On the other hand, contact between people of the same sex is permitted. Men may hold hands with men or even walk with their arms around each other; this is interpreted as nothing except friendship.

- Among both Muslims and Hindus, the left hand is considered unclean. Eat with your right hand only. Where possible, do not touch anything or anyone with your left hand if you can use your right hand instead. Accept gifts and hold cash in the right hand. (Obviously, when both hands are needed, use them both.)

- The foot is also considered unclean. Do not move anything with your feet, do not point with your feet, and do not touch anything with your feet. Feet should not be rested on tables or desks.

- Do not show the soles of your feet or shoes. This restriction determines how one sits: you can cross your legs at the knee but not with one ankle on your knee.

- Pounding one fist into the palm of your other hand is an obscene gesture among some Indonesians.

- The head is considered the seat of the soul by many Indonesians. Never touch someone's head, not even to pat the hair of a child.

- As in much of the world, to beckon someone, you hold your hand out, palm downward, and make a scooping motion with the fingers. Beckoning someone with the palm up and wagging one finger can be construed as an insult.

- It is impolite to point with your forefinger. Point with your right thumb and a closed fist (like a hitchhiker). This gesture is also used to mean "you go first."

- Standing tall with your hands on your hips—the "arms akimbo" position—is always interpreted as an angry, aggressive posture. Indeed, this position is used as a ritualized symbol of anger in the Indonesian *wayang* (shadow puppet) theater.

Gifts

- Gift giving is a traditional part of Indonesian culture. Although gifts may be small, they are often exchanged.

- Gifts can celebrate virtually any occasion: when you return from a trip, when you are invited to an Indonesian home, when a visitor comes to tour your office or workplace, and in return for services rendered.

- It is not customary to unwrap a gift in the presence of the giver. To do so would suggest that the recipient is greedy and impatient. Worse, if the gift is somehow inappropriate or disappointing, it would embarrass both parties. Expect the recipient to thank you briefly, then put the still-wrapped gift aside until you have left.

- Food makes a good gift for most occasions. When a person visits an area of Indonesia where a delicacy is available, he or she is expected to bring some back for friends.

- Pork and alcohol are prohibited to observing Muslims, so do not give them as gifts to Indonesians. Other foods may be appropriate, although meat products must be halal (the Muslim equivalent of kosher). The prohibition against pork and alcohol also precludes pigskin products and perfumes containing alcohol.

- Muslim Indonesians consider dogs unclean. Do not give toy dogs or gifts with pictures of dogs.

- Pets that are prized by Indonesians include cats and birds, especially songbirds. Recordings of the songs of champion songbirds are distributed, and may make a good gift for an Indonesian bird fancier.

- Remember that personal gifts from a man to a woman can be misinterpreted as romantic offerings. When a foreign businessman gives a gift to an Indonesian woman, he must let everyone know that he is simply delivering a gift from his company, or his wife.

- For information on gift giving to ethnically Chinese contacts, see the chapter on China.

- Observant Hindus do not eat beef or use cattle products. This eliminates most leather products as appropriate gifts.

Dress

- Indonesia straddles the Equator, and thus is hot and humid all year long. Most of the lowlands have a daytime temperature range of 75 to 95°F, and humidity around 75 percent.

- Lower temperatures occur only in the mountainous areas.

- The rainy season runs from September through February, but sudden showers occur all year long. Some people carry an umbrella every day.
- Because of the heat and humidity, business dress in Indonesia is often casual. Standard formal office wear for men is dark trousers and a light-colored long-sleeved shirt and tie, without a jacket. Many businessmen wear a short-sleeved shirt with no tie.

  Businesswomen wear long-sleeved blouses, skirts, business suits, and more recently, pantsuits. The colors should by dark and muted; bright, vivid colors are not appropriate for a businesswoman.
- As a foreigner, you should dress more conservatively until you are sure what degree of formality is expected. Men should expect to wear a suit jacket and tie, and remove them if it seems appropriate. Whatever you wear, try to stay clean and well groomed—which is a feat in the tropics.
- Many Indonesian men wear an open-necked batik shirt to work. This is also popular for casual attire. Jeans are good for casual wear, but shorts should be avoided.

  In deference to Muslim and Hindu sensibilities, women should always wear blouses that cover at least their upper arms. Skirts should be knee-length or longer.

Cultural Note

Three calendars are in common use in Indonesia. The Western (or Gregorian) calendar is the official calendar. Islamic holidays are dated by the Arabic calendar, which loses approximately eleven days each year against the Western calendar. In addition, there is a Hindu-influenced Javanese calendar.

When certain days from different calendars coincide, it is considered lucky. For example, when the fifth day of the Western week falls on the fifth day of the Javanese week (which is only five days long), the occasion is considered auspicious.

Japan

Japan

> **Cultural Note**
>
> The term "Japan Inc." has often been used to describe the totality of Japanese business: the tight government control; the huge, interlocking corporate alliances; the hard-working salary men who began each day by singing the company song and getting lifetime employment in return for their loyalty; the postwar Japanese economic miracle. But "Japan Inc." was always an exaggeration, and a decade of poor economic performance has just about ended the myth.
>
> However, business is still conducted differently in Japan than in North America or the EU. The Japanese still prefer to do business in a network of old friends, facilitated by favors and obligations.

▶ WHAT'S YOUR CULTURAL IQ?

1. TRUE or FALSE? Within a generation or two, Japan may have its first female emperor.

   ANSWER: TRUE. Although Japan has historically had male emperors, there has not been a male born into the Japanese royal family for some forty years. The current heir to the throne, Crown Prince Naruhito, has a daughter as his heir, which may force the change in tradition.

2. More than fifty-five years after the end of the Second World War, one of the following Japanese islands remains occupied by a foreign power. Which one is it?
   a. Hokkaido
   b. Kurile Islands
   c. Okinawa

   ANSWER: b) As of this writing, Russia remains in control of the Kurile Islands, which the Japanese refer to as the Northern Territories. Russia's refusal to return the islands is the reason

Japan has never signed a formal peace treaty ending the Second World War with Russia (or with its predecessor, the USSR). Although the USA maintains a controversial military base on Okinawa, it returned the island itself to Japanese control.

3. The Japanese have at least ten distinct breeds of dogs. TRUE or FALSE? The Japanese Tosa makes a fine lap dog for the many Japanese who live in small apartments.
   ANSWER: FALSE. The Tosa is a large dog, originally bred for dog fighting and nicknamed the "Japanese Mastiff." The lap dog bred for upper-class Japanese ladies is the Chin.

▶ TIPS ON DOING BUSINESS IN JAPAN

- A "poker face" is of great use in Japan. The Japanese dislike strong public displays of emotion. If you show shock or anger during business negotiations, they will believe that you lack self-control and are questionable as a business partner.
- The Japanese negotiate in groups, usually in a team containing executives of different age ranges. Your team should have at least one senior member, and everyone must be sure to treat him with deference.
- The younger members of your team should generally remain quiet and defer to their seniors during the meetings. Their real job will be to go out drinking with the Japanese team's young executives at night. The Japanese like to convey important information (e.g., "Our boss was very angry at your offer today") via junior executives.
- It is useful to get Japanese executives away from their home base. In Japan, they can wait you out, hoping that you will agree to a disadvantageous deal because you are anxious to go home. The Japanese often agree to hold negotiations at a midway point. For example, when negotiating with North Americans, the Japanese often agree to hold meetings in Hawaii.
- Hard-sell techniques will fail in Japan. Instead, find the points on which you and your Japanese counterparts agree, then build upon those. A positive, persuasive presentation works better with the Japanese than does a high-pressure, confrontational approach.

- The Japanese may ask international visitors many questions—
  including information about your job, your title, your age, your
  responsibilities, the number of employees that report to you, etc.
  Japanese is a complex language with many forms of address and
  honorifics. They need a lot of information in order to decide which
  form to use when speaking to you. (Most of this subtlety will be lost
  when translated into English, but it is important to the Japanese.)

Cultural Note

Japan is deficient in many important resources, especially petroleum. One of the reasons the
Japanese attacked the Western powers in the Pacific in the Second World War was to secure
supplies of petroleum from Dutch Indonesia. Japan remains an importer of petroleum, and
any disruption of oil supplies causes instability in the Japanese economy.

▶ COUNTRY BACKGROUND

Demographics
Japan's population is approximately 127 million (2006 estimate).
This dense population is cited as the prevailing factor explaining the
Japanese "group mentality." The following statistics are useful for under-
standing just how crowded Japan is: Its land represents only 0.3 percent
of the world's land mass, yet its people represent 3 percent of the world's
population. Over 99 percent of the population consists of native-born
Japanese. The largest minority (less than 1 percent) are Koreans.

History
The Japanese Islands have been occupied for thousands of years.
The dynasty of the current emperor is said to have been founded in
660 B.C.

Historically, Japan has resisted outside influences and frequently
closed itself to foreigners. The United States of America forcibly
opened Japan to foreign markets in 1853 when Commodore Perry
sailed his war fleet into Tokyo Bay.

What Westerners consider World War II was only part of a long-
running Asiatic war in which Japan invaded neighboring nations.

Korea was annexed in 1910, Manchuria was annexed in 1931, and China proper was invaded in 1937.

Japan surrendered to the Allies in 1945, and was occupied until 1952. The USA, wishing to demilitarize and democratize Japan, imposed many reforms after World War II. These efforts included a decrease in the power of the emperor and decentralization of the government. Subsequently, the Japanese recentralized much of their government. Japan's bureaucracy of civil servants became just as powerful (if not more) than its elected officials.

Devastated by the war, the Japanese rebuilt their factories and infrastructure. Japan's economy boomed in the 1970s and 1980s. During this time, cash-rich Japanese bought property and businesses all over the world. This boom ended in the 1990s.

Since then, the Japanese economy has largely been in a state of stagnation. Unable to continue providing traditional lifetime employment, many Japanese workers were laid off. This breaking of the postwar social contract has caused a major change of attitude among many Japanese.

Recently, the government led by Prime Minister Junichiro Koizumi has made some painful changes to the economy. While this resulted in economic improvement in 2003, it remains to be seen if this recovery will be sustained.

Cultural Note

Both foreign and domestic companies are expected to offer apologies for wrongdoing in Japan. In October of 2004 Japan's bank regulatory department, the Financial Services Agency, ordered Citigroup to close its private banking business for fraudulent transactions. Citigroup subsequently flew the company's chief executive officer to Japan to hold a press conference. During the conference, he bowed deeply and apologized for his company's "failure to comply with legal and regulatory requirements in Japan." His apology was broadcast on Japanese television, and it was viewed as an important first step in repairing its reputation with regulators and customers.

Type of Government

Japan is a parliamentary democracy under a constitutional monarch. The chief of state is the emperor; Emperor Akihito was crowned in 1990 after the death of his father, Emperor Hirohito. The head of the government is the prime minister.

Power within the government resides mainly in the prime minister, who is the leader of the majority party of the Diet, or Parliament. The prime minister dissolves the House of Representatives every two or three years. The prime minister also appoints the Supreme Court and leads the Cabinet.

The Diet is made up of two houses, the House of Representatives and the House of Councilors. Both are elected, with the House of Representatives having more authority. Finally, the Cabinet is responsible to the Diet. In the Cabinet, it is the Ministry of Finance (MOF) and the Ministry of International Trade and Industry (MITI) that are the most important.

MITI, through involvement in business and industry following the Second World War, helped Japan gain its strength. Today MITI does not have the same authority it once did, both because it is not as needed as much as before and because of pressure from other governments (such as the United States of America). The government does not control industry; government ministries instead serve as intermediaries and as think tanks.

For current government data, visit the Embassy of Japan at *www .us.emb-japan.go.jp.*

Cultural Note
Japanese uses not one but three different forms of writing: kanji, katakana, and hiragana. As a rule, kanji represents blocks of meaning. Katakana is used for foreign names and words. Hiragana expresses the grammatical relationships between words.

As a foreigner, your name and your company's name will probably be written in katakana characters.

Language
Japanese is the official language of Japan. It is a complex and subtle language, spoken nowhere else in the world as a primary tongue. Most sentences in Japanese can be expressed in at least four different

levels of politeness. Japanese women almost always use one of the more deferential forms. Communication in Japan is often marked by great subtlety; information is left unspoken yet is perfectly understood.

Ethnologue.com has identified fifteen languages currently spoken in Japan. These range from Korean (with some 670,000 speakers) to Ainu (with just 15 active speakers).

Cultural Note

Literacy is close to 100 percent in Japan, and 95 percent of the population has a high school education. The Japanese educational system includes difficult qualifying exams that students must pass, which puts enormous pressure to study and to get good grades. Once a student has passed the entrance exam for college, however, exams are over. Students accepted to the top colleges are almost guaranteed top jobs.

All Japanese students begin classes in English around age twelve. However, the goal for students of English is to pass their exams rather than to learn to verbally communicate in English. Although many Japanese learn to read English, fewer are able to speak with English-speaking foreigners.

Reflecting the increased influence of China, some Japanese are now studying Mandarin Chinese as their second foreign language.

The Japanese View

The Japanese have a unique culture and language. Despite increasing scientific evidence, many Japanese believe that they are genetically unique as well. (One good way to make yourself unpopular in Japan is to quote studies that indicate the Japanese are descended from immigrants from mainland Asia.) Foreign pharmaceuticals are often prohibited in Japan on the basis that they have not been proven to be safe and effective for the Japanese people.

Wherever the Japanese originated, they are extremely protective of their culture and their society. They discourage large numbers of foreigners from coming to work and live in Japan. Even Korean workers who have lived in Japan for several generations are not accorded full citizenship. Foreigners in Japan are often considered to be the source of crime and public disorder.

The prejudice against foreigners can even be directed at native-born Japanese. Often, Japanese who spend too much time studying abroad are stigmatized for "not being Japanese enough."

One important aspect of Japanese behavior is apology. Not only do individuals apologize for missteps, but companies do as well (in the person of their highest-ranking officers).

Japan has its own unique belief system, called Shinto. Shinto means "the way of the gods," yet it is not always categorized by Westerners as a religion, in part because Shinto lacks an official religious text or a system of ethics to live by.

The Japanese are surprisingly tolerant of religious differences, and may even practice both Buddhism and Shinto concurrently. Many people are married in a Shinto ceremony but select a Buddhist funeral.

Cultural Note

Like many industrialized countries, Japan has had a declining birth rate. Japan's population is expected to begin shrinking by 2007. Efforts by the Japanese government to encourage citizens to have more children—including tax breaks and maternity leave—have failed to halt the decline. The low birthrate will lead to a dearth of young workers by 2050. Because there will be fewer workers contributing to government social insurance programs, this is expected to cause severe problems. It may even force the Japanese to allow guest workers to enter Japan.

Christianity (less than 5 percent) and other religions (under 20 percent) are also present in Japan. There is no official religion. The Japanese tend to adapt their religion to modern life; for example, they will have new businesses blessed. Another change is in the view of suicide. Suicide was accepted in older Japanese traditions whenever one had brought intolerable shame upon oneself. The official policy in Japan today is to discourage suicide. Nevertheless, Japan has a high suicide rate. Despite a martial history, Japan has not had an army since the end of the Second World War. The 2003 decision to send some 500 members of Japan's Self-Defense Forces to aid in the occupation and reconstruction of Iraq was very controversial. The majority of Japanese opposed the presence of Japanese troops in Iraq.

☑ Know Before You Go

The greatest difficulty for foreigners involves finding one's way about. Most signs are only in Japanese (some tourist attractions and large avenues have multilingual signs). Not all buildings have street numbers. The layout of most cities is chaotic and confusing. Efforts to use public transportation are often made difficult by impatient crowds. Unless they have a guide, first-time visitors to Japan are often overwhelmed.

Japan is one of the most tectonically active nations in the world. The country has suffered many devastating earthquakes. It also has several active volcanoes: Mt. Usu on Hokkaido erupted in April 2000. Visitors to Japan should know that they may be viewed with suspicion in the aftermath of a natural disaster; foreigners have often been blamed for "causing disruption" (i.e., looting) after earthquakes.

Japan is also occasionally the victim of destructive typhoons or tsunamis.

North Americans should know that they are, on average, larger (both taller and wider) than the average Japanese. Consequently, they may find Japanese accommodations (everything from shower stalls to train seats) difficult to use. You may also find it difficult to purchase clothes in your size.

Japan has occasionally experienced terrorist attacks. The Red Brigade carried out attacks in the 1970s. More recently, in 1995, a religious sect released the deadly nerve gas sarin on the Tokyo subway, causing a dozen deaths and injuring thousands.

Open prejudice against foreigners is occasionally encountered in Japan. You may be told that certain services are "for Japanese only," especially when you travel outside areas frequented by tourists.

Japanese taxi drivers are notoriously erratic, and can be a danger to both pedestrians and other drivers.

If you are staying in Japan and are considering buying a car, realize that the purchase price is only part of your costs. In addition to insurance, you must first rent a registered parking space for your car. Old cars are sold very cheaply because they require expensive repairs to pass inspection (this is one reason all the cars in Japan look so well maintained).

Cultural Note

Japan has a long literary history. A work from the eighth century A.D. called the *Manyoshu* (Collection of 10,000 Leaves) contains Japanese poetry that many feel has never been equaled.

The Japanese added Western literary forms to their repertoire after the opening of Japan in 1853. The first Japanese novel is *Ukigumo* (The Drifting Cloud), which appeared in installments from 1887 to 1889. Written by Futabatei Shimei, it also introduced the concept of the antihero to Japanese literature. (*continued*)

Akutagawa Ryunosuke became world famous for his short story "Rashomon," in which a single incident is retold from the point of view of different participants. This story has been adapted into a play and made into a film.

Among postwar authors, Yukio Mishima most captured the imagination of the Western community. (*Time* magazine called him "the Hemingway of Japan.") Fiercely nationalistic, he advocated the remilitarization of Japan, and ended his own life via traditional seppuku (ritual disembowelment).

▶ CULTURAL ORIENTATION

Cognitive Styles: How Japanese Organize and Process Information

The Japanese generally close all doors to outside influences, although they are open to ideas from within their group. They are subjective and experiential in their thinking, holding fast to traditional values. Strong loyalty to their groups makes the Japanese look to the particular and specific rather than the universal and abstract. While the Japanese pride themselves on anticipating others' needs, they can also be very compartmentalized.

Negotiation Strategies: What Japanese Accept as Evidence

The Japanese may rely more on their feelings than on facts, because they tend to be more subjective than objective. Since they strive for consensus within their groups, individuals are prepared to change their position for the sake of group harmony.

Foreigners sometimes interpret the Japanese dismissal of facts and decision-by-consensus process as evidence that the Japanese believe that they are superior to others. The opaqueness of their decision-making and their tightly controlled communicative behavior exacerbates this situation with unknowing foreigners.

Value Systems: The Basis for Behavior

Traditional Japanese value systems have recently eroded due to the failure of the postwar social compact (especially the loss of lifetime employment). These views are especially prevalent among the younger generation. The following three sections identify the Value

Systems in the predominant culture—their methods of dividing right from wrong, good from evil, and so forth.

Locus of Decision-Making

Decisions are made within the group with little or no recognition. A person's actions reflect on the group, particularly his or her family. Outsiders must be accepted into the group before they can participate in decision-making. The Japanese are only moderately collective.

Sources of Anxiety Reduction

The Japanese have very high anxiety about life because of the need to avoid embarrassment. There are constant pressures to conform. A very strong work ethic and strong group relationships give structure and stability to life. Emotional restraints are developed in childhood, and all behaviors are situation-bound. This makes it extremely difficult for a foreigner to understand the culture.

Issues of Equality/Inequality

Age is revered. There is a great deal of competitiveness among equals, but also an inherent trust in people. Ethnocentrism is very strong. Male dominance is still strong in public situations. Gender roles in society are clearly differentiated, but a desire for Western-style equality is growing among Japanese youth.

Cultural Note

Japanese politics, like most areas of power, has been almost exclusively male for decades. Recently this has begun to change.

In February 2000, Fusae Ota became the first Japanese woman to win a gubernatorial election when she became governor of Osaka. She was a former officer in the powerful Ministry of International Trade and Industry (known as MITI).

▶ BUSINESS PRACTICES

Punctuality, Appointments, and Local Time

- Be punctual at all times. Tardiness is considered rude.

- The work week is generally forty-eight hours without overtime pay, spread over five and a half working days. Some large firms have instituted a five-day week. While the Japanese work long hours, few executives take their work home with them.
- During holidays, banks and offices close, although some stores remain open.
- For a list of the official holidays of Japan, visit *www.kissbowor shakehands.com*.
- During three weeks of the year (New Year's holidays, December 28 to January 3; Golden Week, April 29 to May 5; and Obon, in mid-August), many people visit the graves of their ancestors. Conducting business and traveling are difficult during these periods.
- When writing the date in English, the Japanese may write the year first, then the month, then the day (e.g., December 3, 2010, would be 10.12.3 or 10/12/3) or they may write the day first, then the month, then the year (e.g., December 3, 2010, would be written 3.12.10).
- Japan is nine hours ahead of Greenwich Mean Time (G.M.T. + 9), or fourteen hours ahead of Eastern Standard Time (E.S.T. + 14).

Cultural Note

The Japanese also have a non-Western method of designating the year: they use the year of the current emperor's reign. This year is now considered to begin on the first of January in the Gregorian (Western) calendar.

The New Year is the most important holiday in Japan. Businesses close for three to five days. Many people send greeting cards to celebrate. *Bonekai* parties ("year forget parties") are held to put all of the old year's worries to rest. People visit shrines, eat specific foods, and even play obscure games, such as *hanetsuki*, a Japanese form of badminton.

Negotiating

- A Japanese response "I'll consider it" may actually mean "no."
- Negatively phrased questions typically get a "yes" if the Japanese speaker agrees. For example, a question such as "Doesn't Company A want us?" will be answered "yes" if the Japanese thinks

that Company A indeed does not want you. In English, the answer would be "No, they do not want you."

- Incorporate the words "I'm sorry" into your vocabulary when you go to Japan. However, don't be ingratiating out of fear of offending; just be polite.
- Negotiations are begun at the executive level and continued at the middle level (working level).
- Connections are very helpful in Japan. However, choose your intermediaries carefully, because the Japanese will feel obliged to be loyal to them. Do not choose someone of lower rank than the person with whom he or she will be negotiating. Intermediaries should not be part of either company involved in the deal.
- If you don't have a connection, a personal call is better than a letter or e-mail.
- Use an intermediary to convey bad news.
- Using a Japanese lawyer rather than a Western one indicates a cooperative spirit.
- The Japanese usually use the initial meetings to get to know you, while at the same time asking to hear about your proposal. Agreements of confidentiality are vague.
- Contracts are not perceived as final agreements. You or they may renegotiate.
- Because age equals rank, show the greatest respect to the oldest members of the Japanese group with whom you are in contact.
- You will not be complimented on good work, because the group and not the individual is rewarded. It is a bad idea to single out Japanese workers.
- The Japanese will not explain exactly what is expected of you.
- Most Japanese go through job rotation, in which they change jobs within the same company every few years. In this way, the employees get to know the company and its workforce well.
- Suggestion boxes, so often ignored in the USA, are useful in Japan, because Japanese employees stuff them full of suggestions.
- Do not make accusations or refuse anything directly; be indirect.
- At work the Japanese are very serious and do not try to "lighten things up" with humor.

- When working with Japanese who know English, or when using an interpreter, be patient. Speak slowly, pause often, and avoid colloquialisms. Your interpreter may seem to be taking more time with the translation than you did with your statement; this is because she or he is using lengthy forms of respect.
- Do not be surprised if your interpreter translates Japanese into English almost simultaneously, but waits until English speakers are finished before translating into Japanese. Unlike English, Japanese is a very predictable language. By the time a Japanese businessperson is halfway through a sentence, the translator probably knows how the sentence will end. Indeed, it would be very impolite of a Japanese to end a sentence with an unexpected choice of words.
- At times, you may need to pretend you are sure that your Japanese colleague or friend has understood you, even if you know this is not the case. This is important for maintaining a good relationship.

Cultural Note

Asian psychology requires that people observe the proper order of things. When three Japanese hostages were released from Iraq in 2004, they had to pay for their own flights home. Instead of being welcomed back to Japan, they returned to widespread animosity because they had entered Iraq against their government's recommendation. This was a violation of protocol, and they were perceived to have put the government and the Japanese people in a bad position.

Business Entertaining

- Business entertaining usually occurs after business hours, and very rarely in the home. You will be entertained often, sometimes on short notice. While the first evenings will probably be spent going from bar to restaurant to "hostess bar" (not a good idea for businesswomen), you may suggest alternatives later. These may include sumo wrestling or karaoke ("empty orchestra") bars, where you sing along with pre-recorded music.
- When you are taken out, your host will treat.
- Allow your host to order for you (this will be easier, too, since the menus are in Japanese). Be enthusiastic while eating, and express your thanks afterward.

- While business entertaining is primarily for building friendships rather than for making deals, you may discuss business during the evening.
- If you are invited to a Japanese home, keep in mind that this is a great honor: show your appreciation.
- For social occasions, it is appropriate to be fashionably late.
- When entering a Japanese home, take off your shoes at the door. You will wear one pair of slippers from the door to the living room, where you will remove them. You will put them on again to make your way to the bathroom, where you will exchange them for "toilet slippers." Do not forget to change back again.
- In a home, you will sit cross-legged, or with your legs to the side, around a low table with the family. You may be offered a backrest.
- Meals are long, but the evening usually ends at about 11:00 P.M.
- Never point your chopsticks at another person. When you are not using them, you should line them up on the chopstick rest.
- Use both hands to hold a bowl or a cup that you wish to be refilled.
- Eventually, you will wish to invite your hosts out. Be insistent, even if they claim that a foreigner should not pay for anything.

Cultural Note

Good topics of conversation include families (yours and your Japanese counterpart's), Japanese art and inventiveness, Japanese hospitality, and sports. Popular sports in Japan include baseball, ski jumping, and (since the World Cup was hosted in Japan and South Korea) football (soccer). Avoid bringing up the Second World War or Japanese militarism in general.

⊙ PROTOCOL

Greetings

- The Japanese are very aware of Western habits and will often greet you with a handshake. Their handshakes will often be gentle; this gives no indication of their assertiveness of character.
- The handshake may last longer than customary in northern Europe or North America.

- The bow is their traditional greeting.
- If someone bows to greet you, observe carefully. If you are greeting an equal, bow to the same depth as you have been bowed to, because the depth of the bow indicates the status of the relationship between you. As you bow, quickly lower your eyes. Keep your palms flat against your thighs.

Cultural Note

Business cards are extremely important for establishing credentials. Have them prepared in advance and checked by a Japanese business representative. It is best to have one side printed in your native language, with extra information such as membership in professional associations included; the reverse side should be in Japanese. If your status changes, have new cards printed immediately.

Cards are presented after the bow or handshake. Present your card with the Japanese side facing your colleague, in such a manner that it can be read immediately.

Read the card presented to you, memorizing all the information. Ask for help in pronunciation and in comprehension of the title; if you understand without help, make a relevant comment. Handle cards very carefully. Do not put them in your pocket or in your wallet if you plan to put it in your back pocket. Never write on a person's business card (especially not in his or her presence).

Titles/Forms of Address

- In person, use last names plus *San*, meaning "Mr." or "Ms." Do not immediately assume that the Japanese will call you by your first name.
- In correspondence, it is more respectful to add *–dono* or *–sama* to the last name.
- Titles are important in Japan. Appendix A contains several equivalent translations of titles such as President and COO in Japanese.

Gestures

- Japan is a high-context culture; even the smallest gesture carries great meaning. Therefore, avoid expansive arm and hand movements, unusual facial expressions, or dramatic gestures.
- The American "okay" sign (thumb and forefinger curled in an O) means "money" to the Japanese.

- Some Western gestures convey nothing to the Japanese. These include a shrug of the shoulders or a wink between friends.
- Pointing is considered impolite. Instead, wave your hand, palm up, toward the object being indicated, as the Japanese do.
- Beckoning "come here" is done with the palm down.
- Moving the open hand, with the palm facing left, in a fanning motion in front of the face indicates a negative response.
- Sniffing, snorting, and spitting in public are acceptable, but nose blowing is not. When you must blow your nose, use a disposable tissue and then throw it out.
- To get through a crowd, the Japanese may push others. There is also a gesture meaning "excuse me," which involves repeating a bow and a karate chop in the air.
- The Japanese do not approve of male-female touching in public.
- Men do not engage in backslapping or other forms of touching.
- In conversation, the Japanese remain farther apart than do North Americans.
- Prolonged direct eye contact is not the norm.
- A smile can mean pleasure, but it can also be a means of self-control, as when it is used to hide disapproval or anger.
- Keep a smile, even when you are upset.
- Laughter can mean embarrassment, confusion, or shock, rather than mirth.
- Silence is considered useful.

Cultural Note
Should you have occasion to visit a Japanese person who is ill, never bring him or her white flowers. The color white is associated with death. Also, avoid giving a potted plant, which suggests that the sick person will soon be planted in the ground.

Gifts
- If you are invited to a Japanese home, bring flowers, cakes, or candy.
- Gift giving is very common in Japan. Business gifts absolutely must be given at midyear (July 15) and at year-end (January 1). They are often given at first business meetings.

- For the Japanese, the ceremony of gift giving is more important than the objects exchanged. Do not be surprised by either modest or extravagant gifts.
- Take your cue from the Japanese with whom you are working. Allow them to present gifts first, and make your gift of the same quality as theirs.
- The Japanese do not usually open gifts directly upon receipt. If they do, they will be restrained in their appreciation. This does not mean that they do not like your present. Again, follow their lead.
- Good gifts are imported Scotch, cognac, or frozen steaks; electronic gadgets and toys for children of associates; or items made by well-known manufacturers. Elite, foreign name-brands are always best.
- Always wrap your gifts in Japan or have them wrapped by hotel or store services. It is best to buy the paper there, so as not to choose a paper that is considered tasteful in your home country but unattractive in Japan (for example, black and white paper is unacceptable). Rice paper is ideal.
- Avoid giving gifts with even numbers of components, such as an even number of flowers in a bouquet. Four is an especially inauspicious number; never give four of anything.

Cultural Note
While you should expect to dress formally while in Japan, you can leave your handkerchief at home. Carry small facial tissues rather than a handkerchief. The Japanese consider the Western practice of blowing their nose into a piece of cloth, then folding up that cloth and preserving it in a pocket, to be grotesque. When a Japanese person blows his nose, he does so into a disposable tissue and throws the tissue away immediately.

Dress
- Men should wear conservative suits. Avoid casual dress in any business meeting.
- Because shoes are removed frequently, many people wear shoes that slip on.

- Women should dress conservatively, keeping jewelry, perfume, and makeup to a minimum. Pants are becoming more common. High heels are to be avoided if you risk towering over your Japanese counterparts.
- Summer is usually very hot in Japan, so bring lightweight cotton clothing. Be sure to have plenty of changes of attire, because the Japanese are very concerned with neatness.
- If you wear a kimono, wrap it left over right! Only corpses wear them wrapped right over left.

Cultural Note

The Japanese are very fond of their pets, even though they can be rather unusual. Japanese pets include octopi, wild birds, ants (in ant farms), and singing insects.

However, they also like "conventional" pets, and have some 7 million cats and 9½ million dogs. To avoid the tragedy of dogs or cats running away, Japanese companies have radio-tracking devices small enough to be placed in a pet's collar, and ID chips under their skin. One company markets a miniature global positioning system receiver for dogs!

Malaysia

Former name: Federation of Malaysia

▶ WHAT'S YOUR CULTURAL IQ?

1. Malaysia was a colony until after the Second World War. TRUE or FALSE: Before the Japanese occupation, Malaysia was owned by the Netherlands.
   ANSWER: FALSE. Malaysia was a colony of the United Kingdom. Neighboring Indonesia was owned by the Dutch.

2. Malaysia shares which large island with two other nations?
   a. Borneo
   b. Java
   c. Sumatra
   ANSWER: a. The island of Borneo is shared by Malaysia, Indonesia, and the Sultanate of Brunei.

3. Malaysia is rich in natural resources and has developed a formidable manufacturing capacity. Which of the following does Malaysia produce?
   a. Computer disk drives
   b. Timber

c. Protons
d. Rubber
e. All of the above

ANSWER: e. *c* does not refer to subatomic particles—"Proton" is the name of a car.

▶ TIPS ON DOING BUSINESS IN MALAYSIA

- Keep in mind that Malaysia is the only country in Southeast Asia that is divided between the Asian mainland and an archipelago. It shares the Malay Peninsula with Thailand. Business and politics are affected by events in adjacent countries. For example, Malaysia was very concerned about the treatment of ethnic Malays in southern Thailand in 2004.

- In Malaysia, a smile is not the ubiquitous gesture that Westerners may expect. People in Malaysia may smile or laugh to hide embarrassment, shyness, bitterness, or discord. Malaysian businessmen may laugh during the most serious part of a business meeting; this may be an expression of anxiety, not frivolity.

- In multicultural Malaysia, it is good business to know something about each of the three main ethnic groups—Malay, Indian, and Chinese. Ethnic Malays, called *Bumiputera*, comprise the majority of Malaysia's government. The educated Indian population will generally be in a variety of professions, such as lawyers and journalists. The largest percentage of Malaysian businesspeople are Chinese.

- Although the Chinese and Indians are immigrants to Malaysia, do not assume they are newcomers. The Chinese began arriving in the fifteenth century! While many Indians came to Malaysia after World War I, it was Indian traders who brought Islam to Malaysia—over 400 years ago. There is a good chance that a Chinese or Indian person's ancestors were in Malaysia long before the United States of America declared independence.

- Remember to follow the taboos typical of Islamic societies: eat only with your right hand (because the left hand is considered unclean), never expose the soles of your feet, dress modestly, and avoid alcohol and pork products.

▶ COUNTRY BACKGROUND

Demographics

Ethnic Malays make up just over 60 percent of the Malaysian population. Ethnic Chinese constitute almost 30 percent, and ethnic Indians number over 9 percent. The remainder constitutes a wide variety of native and foreign peoples. Consequently, Malaysia's population of approximately 24 million (a 2006 estimate) is divided not only by geography but by race and language as well.

History

The proto-Malay people reached Malaysia thousands of years ago. Some of their modern-day descendants still live in the jungles of Borneo, where their traditional cultures have scarcely changed. There are also some 100,000 non-Malay aboriginal people; the Semang and Pangan.

Malaysia has long been a center of international trade. The country lies directly on the sea routes between China and India. For centuries, small kingdoms and sultanates in what is now Malaysia profited from this trade, either by assisting it or by preying upon it. In the sixteenth century, Europeans began trading in Asia. Trade bases were established, and the Malay "pirate kingdoms" were gradually conquered. Malaysia became a British colony.

The British were temporarily driven out by the Japanese during World War II. In 1946, faced with the nationalist aspirations of the Malay peoples, the British consolidated the patchwork of sultanates and states on the Malay Peninsula into a crown colony called the Malayan Union. The sultans were deprived of power, and all citizens were given equal rights.

Many ethnic Malays were dissatisfied with the Malayan Union. Some wished to restore the powers of their Islamic sultans. Furthermore, the Chinese minority had always been the most wealthy and educated ethnic group on the Malay Peninsula. The ethnic Malays, despite their numerical majority, feared that the aggressive Chinese would take over the new crown colony. (The Chinese-dominated Malayan Communist Party did conduct a guerrilla war against British and Malay forces from 1948 until 1960.)

As a result, the Malayan Union was replaced in 1948 with the Malayan Federation. The sultans were restored to power, and the ethnic Malays were guaranteed favorable treatment. In effect, a balance was established between the Malays and the Chinese: The Malays would run the government, and the Chinese would run the businesses. This division is essentially still in effect today. (The Indian population at that time consisted mostly of poor agricultural laborers. They were not considered in the settlement.)

The Federation of Malaya became independent from the United Kingdom in 1957. A new, expanded nation was proposed, uniting the Malay Peninsula, the island crown colony of Singapore, and the three British-controlled territories on the island of Borneo: Sarawak, Brunei, and North Borneo (later renamed Sabah). The sultan of Brunei, wealthy with oil revenues, declined to join. (Brunei remained a British protectorate until becoming an independent country in 1984.) The other Borneo territories, Sarawak and Sabah, joined the new federation, as did Singapore.

The new Federation of Malaysia came into being in 1963. Since 1963, the only change in the makeup of the Federation of Malaysia has been the secession of Singapore in 1965.

Cultural Note

The word "Malay" has several meanings. It can refer to the Malay linguistic group; Malaysia's official language, Bahasa Malaysia, is a standardized form of Malay (similar but not identical to Bahasa Indonesia). Malay can also refer to the dominant ethnic group of Malaysia. Finally, Malay has a geographic meaning; the peninsula shared by Thailand and West Malaysia is called the Malay Peninsula.

Geopolitically, several variants were used by the British during the colonial and postcolonial era: first Malaya, then the Malayan Union, and later the Federation of Malaya. The current nation was formed on September 16, 1963, with the name the Federation of Malaysia. The citizens of Malaysia are Malaysians, while the Malays are the dominant ethnic group in Malaysia.

Type of Government

Malaysia is a constitutional monarchy. The monarchy is rather unique: the nine hereditary sultans elect from among themselves a "paramount ruler" for a five-year term. The paramount ruler—essentially a king with a five-year reign—is the chief of state of Malaysia. "Paramount ruler" is the English term; the actual Malay title is *Yang di-Pertuan Agong*.

The head of government of Malaysia is the prime minister. The United Malays National Organization (UMNO) is the most powerful political party. There are two legislative houses: the Senate and the House of Representatives.

Current government data can be found at Malaysia's Web site of their embassies worldwide at *www.my.embassyinformation.com*.

Cultural Note

Malaysia experienced tremendous economic growth under the leadership of Prime Minister Mahathir Mohamad. His New Economic Policy brought millions of Malaysians out of subsistence agriculture and into the working class. He and his UMNO Party proposed a New Development Policy designed to put at least 30 percent of Malaysia's wealth into the hands of ethnic Malays—a direct challenge to Chinese economic domination. And his "Vision 2020" plan called for Malaysia to be a fully developed nation by the year 2020.

But Mahathir was also a polarizing figure during his twenty-two-year reign. He instituted draconian laws covering many areas of life and allowed those laws to be used against his political opponents. (The world was stunned when Mahathir's expected successor, Deputy Prime Minister Anwar Ibrahim, fell out of favor and faced trial. He was sentenced to six years for corruption and nine years for sodomy!) Mahathir blamed international currency speculators for the Asian financial crisis that ended Malaysia's economic boom in 1997. And he clearly favored ethnic Malays over the other ethnic groups in his country.

Language

The official language of Malaysia is Bahasa Malaysia, which evolved out of the trade language called Bazaar Malay. It is now written in the Latin alphabet; spelling and orthography were standardized in 1972. Ethnologue.com has identified 140 languages spoken in Malaysia, one of which is now extinct. As a result of British colonialism, the English language is widely understood in Malaysia, and there are many English loan words in Bahasa Malaysia. (This is one of the factors that separates Bahasa Malaysia from Bahasa Indonesia—

Indonesia was a colony of the Netherlands, so Bahasa Indonesia's loan words come from Dutch.) Although English has had a unifying effect on the diverse Malaysian population, the Malaysian authorities have made Bahasa Malaysia the official language of government and education. At home, a Malay family might speak one of several Malay dialects, just as a Chinese family might speak Mandarin or Hakka or Cantonese, or an Indian family speak Tamil or Hindi or Gujarati.

Cultural Note

Islam has long been the predominant religion in Malaysia. Consequently, the use of Arabic script was widespread before the adoption of the Latin alphabet. The Latin alphabet has not entirely replaced Arabic; there are still Malaysian newspapers published in Arabic script. In order to write Bahasa Malaysia in Arabic script, five additional letters must be added to the traditional twenty-eight Arabic letters.

The Malaysian View

Most religions are represented in Malaysia: Islam, Buddhism, Daoism, Hinduism, Christianity, Sikhism, and Shamanism in Eastern Malaysia. Ethnic Malays and some Indians are Muslims. Most Chinese, when forced to choose, will describe themselves as "Buddhist," but they may follow several religious traditions concurrently.

Although Malaysia is officially an Islamic state, nearly half the population identifies itself as non-Muslim.

Former Malaysian Prime Minister Mahathir Mohamad defended Asian traditions in a book he coauthored called *The Voice of Asia*:

Westerners generally cannot rid themselves of (their) sense of superiority. They still consider their values and political and economic systems better than any others. It would not be so bad if it stopped at that; it seems, however, that they will not be satisfied until they have forced other countries to adopt their ways as well. Everyone must be democratic, but only according to the Western concept of democracy; no one can violate human rights, again, according to their self-righteous interpretation of human rights. Westerners cannot seem to understand diversity.

Malaysians obviously feel comfortable with their own cultural traditions and will defend them.

☑ Know Before You Go

Malaysia is close to the epicenter of the tsunami of 2004, but it was shielded from full impact by the island of Sumatra in Indonesia. Besides the tragedy of the earthquakes and tsunamis, the greatest hazards faced by the average foreign traveler are those found in most countries near the equator: sunburn, heat stroke, and/or digestive upsets. Frightening incidents reported in the global news that also occur, but are relatively rare, include: mob violence, typhoons, and floods.

Malaysia maintains some of the strictest censorship laws in the world. It is official policy to insulate the Malaysian population from the "corrupting" foreign media. Foreign journalists are routinely asked to leave the country after writing something uncomplimentary about Malaysia.

Although Malaysia has virtually no Jewish population, anti-Semitism is common, especially among Muslims. Even former Prime Minister Mahathir Mohamad publicly blamed Jews for his country's financial problems.

Bribery and corruption are not unknown in Malaysia. Historically, Malaysia has been considered less corrupt than Indonesia but more corrupt than Singapore (which enforces strict antibribery laws).

▶ CULTURAL ORIENTATION

Cognitive Styles: How Ethnic Malays Organize and Process Information

Although the ethnic Malays have assimilated many indigenous religious rituals into their Islamic religion, they adhere to the closed thinking of Islam when it comes to accepting outside information into their everyday lives. Information is processed subjectively and associatively, and this leads to personal involvement in problems rather than abstract analysis.

Negotiation Strategies: What Ethnic Malays Accept as Evidence

The subjective feelings of the moment form the basis for truth, with faith in the ideologies of Islam having a very strong influence.

Only the most westernized and secular of ethnic Malays will use objective facts as the sole source of the truth.

Value Systems: The Basis for Behavior

Much of the business in Malaysia is conducted by the Chinese and Indians, who have a very different system of values from the ethnic Malays. The following three sections identify the Value Systems in the predominant culture—their methods of dividing right from wrong, good from evil, and so forth.

Locus of Decision-Making

The individual ethnic Malay makes decisions based upon the immediate situation and the relationships among those involved. The highly religious may refer to Islamic guidebooks which detail the proper way to handle every decision in life.

Ethnic Malays are quick to organize and have the support of the group behind their decisions. They are not good at confrontations and try to communicate in such a way as to alleviate conflict. They seldom use a categorical "no." It is important for foreign business executives to develop a personal relationship with their Malaysian counterparts.

Sources of Anxiety Reduction

Solid religious beliefs among ethnic Malays give structure and stability to life. The norm is a nuclear household with strong ties to both the husband's and wife's extended families. The extended family is expected to help in time of need. There is little friction between common law and Islamic law, as they are often combined into a single pronouncement. Respect for authority, unbreakable family ties, and the performance of proper social behavior provide strength in times of stress.

Issues of Equality/Inequality

Most states have sultans, and the division between royalty and commoners is rarely bridged. Royalty is treated with great deference, which includes elaborate ritual and special terms of address. The ethnic Malays hold the political power, but they and the economically dominant Chinese continually joust with each other. Ethnocentrism and stereotypes abound, but virulent racism is stifled. Malaysians practice the strong masculine hierarchy of a secular Muslim state.

Cultural Note

Malaysia has joined a selective core of intellectual property conventions. They include the Berne Convention for Protection of Copyright, the Paris Convention (relative to patents and trademarks), and the Patent Cooperation Treaty. Malaysia has managed to stay out of the spotlight while many of its neighbors have been targeted as pirates and counterfeiters. As a former colony of the United Kingdom, Malaysia carries vestiges of common law trademarks.

▶ BUSINESS PRACTICES

Punctuality, Appointments, and Local Time

- Although most Malays are Muslim, not all of Malaysia follows the traditional Islamic work week pattern (Friday is the Islamic holy day, so the traditional Muslim "weekend" is Thursday and Friday). The Malaysian capital city, Kuala Lumpur, is in the state of Selangor, where the work week is Monday through Friday.
- It is important to be on time for all business appointments. Never make a Malaysian executive wait.
- The majority of Malaysian businesspeople are Chinese; they are likely to be prompt. The majority of government officials are ethnic Malays. Their culture is very different from that of the Chinese, and they have a more flexible concept of time. Although foreigners are expected to be on time, an ethnic Malay may or may not be prompt.
- The Indian minority conception of time is closer to the Malay than to the Chinese. However, the Indians a foreign businessperson is likely to come in contact with are professionals: lawyers, reporters, physicians, and so forth. They will expect punctuality.
- Social events in Malaysia involving different cultural groups have different rules. In general, when invited to a social event, most

Malaysians arrive on time or slightly late. Never be more than a half-hour late.

- A social event hosted by observant Muslims will be without alcohol. There will be no predinner "cocktail hour" and (probably) no appetizers, so the meal may be served close to the time given on the invitation.
- Once a close friendship has been established, guests may arrive a few minutes early to a social occasion. If you are the host and your guests are close friends, it is important to be ready early.
- Try to schedule appointments as early as possible. Malaysian executives are extremely busy. Many travel frequently, especially to conferences in their area of specialization.
- English is the language of many business transactions and correspondence. However, the English spoken often has native inflections, syntax, and grammar, which can easily lead to misunderstandings.
- Bahasa Malaysia is the official language of Malaysia. Although most government officials will speak some English, they may prefer to hold meetings in their native tongue. Fortunately, an English-speaking translator is usually close at hand.
- All official correspondence with government officials must be in Bahasa Malaysia. You may accompany this correspondence with an English translation, if you wish.
- Unlike in nearby Singapore (which has mandated Mandarin Chinese as the official Chinese dialect), Malaysian Chinese often speak mutually unintelligible dialects of Chinese. As a result, the only spoken language a Cantonese-speaking Chinese may have in common with a Hakka-speaking Chinese is English. Similarly, the different linguistic groups within the Indian community often speak English between themselves. English is seen as a unifying force in Malaysia.
- Although lunch has generally been reduced to a single hour (from two hours), Muslims may take a two-hour break on Fridays in order to attend a mosque.
- Executives often work far longer days than their subordinates do. The Chinese, especially, have reputations as workaholics.

- Holidays in Malaysia vary from state to state. The heavily Muslim states do not celebrate any non-Islamic holidays (including Easter, Christmas, and Western New Year's Day). For Malaysia's official holidays, visit *www.kissboworshakehands.com.*
- Malaysians usually write the day first, then the month, then the year (e.g., December 3, 2010, is written 3.12.10 or 3/12/10).
- Malaysia is eight hours ahead of Greenwich Mean Time (G.M.T. + 8), making it thirteen hours ahead of U.S. Eastern Standard Time (E.S.T. + 13).

Negotiating

- Malaysians prefer to do business with persons they know and like. Establishing this personal relationship will take time, but it is vital for success.
- The pace of business negotiations in Malaysia is slower than in the West. Be patient; it would be unusual to complete a complicated business deal in only one visit. Expect to take several trips over a period of months. Indeed, little will happen at the first meeting except getting acquainted.
- Courtesy is the single most important attribute for successful relationships in Malaysia. This civility in no way hinders the determination of Malaysian businesspeople to get their own way.
- Standards of polite behavior vary widely between cultures. Many Malaysians will ask you highly personal questions (such as "Why aren't you married?" or "How much do you earn?") without realizing that Westerners find such questions intrusive. Simply smile and change the topic—and be aware that you, too, will unknowingly violate local standards of polite behavior.
- Because courtesy requires that a Malaysian not disagree openly, the word "no" is rarely heard. A polite but insincere "yes" is simply a technique to avoid giving offense. In Malaysia, "yes" can mean anything from "I agree" to "maybe" to "I hope you can tell from my lack of enthusiasm that I really mean 'no.'"
- "Yes" really means "no" when there are any qualifications attached. "Yes, but . . ." probably means "no." "It might be difficult" is a distinct "no."

- A clear way to indicate "no" is to suck in air through the teeth. This sound always indicates a problem.
- When it comes to making a decision, a "yes" often comes more quickly than a "no." This is because a way must be found to deliver the "no" politely. The "no" may even be delivered through a third party.
- Because Malaysians (especially the Chinese) often consult astrologers, signing a contract may be delayed until an "auspicious" day arrives.
- In Malaysia, as in Indonesia and much of Asia, people who lose their tempers are considered unable to control themselves. Such individuals are not trusted or respected.
- Be cautious in asking Malaysian Chinese a question. English speakers would give a negative answer to the question "Isn't my order ready yet?" by responding "no" (meaning, "No, it's not ready"). The Chinese pattern is the opposite: "yes" (meaning, "Yes, it is not ready.").
- Malaysians of all ethnic groups are comfortable with silence. A silent pause allows time for thought; it does not necessarily signal either acceptance or rejection. Westerners often find such pauses uncomfortable.
- Age and seniority are highly respected. If you are part of a delegation, line up so that the most important persons will be introduced first. If you are introducing two people, state the name of the most important person first (e.g., "President Smith, this is Engineer Wong").
- Business cards should be printed (preferably embossed) in English. The majority of Malaysian businesspeople are ethnic Chinese, so you may wish to have the reverse side of some of your cards translated into Chinese (gold ink is the most prestigious color for Chinese characters). Your business card should contain as much information as possible.
- The exchange of business cards is a formal ceremony in Malaysia. After introductions are made, the visiting businessperson should offer his or her card. Make sure you give a card to each person present. Present your card either with both hands or with your right hand (with the left hand lightly supporting your right). Give your

card to the recipient with the print facing him or her (so the recipient can read it). He or she will receive the card with both hands, then study the card for a few moments before carefully putting it away in a pocket. You should do the same when a card is presented to you. Never put a card in your back pocket (where many men carry their wallets). Do not write on someone's business card.

- Topics to avoid in conversation include any criticism of Malaysian ways, religion, bureaucracy, or politics. Also, avoid any discussion of sex or the roles of the sexes.
- Good topics for discussion include tourism, travel, plans for the future, organizational success (talking about personal success is considered bombastic), and food (while remaining complimentary to the local cuisine).

Cultural Note

Speak in quiet, gentle tones. Always remain calm. Leave plenty of time for someone to respond to a statement you make; people in Malaysia do not jump on the end of one another's sentences. They often leave a respectful pause (as long as ten seconds) before responding. Westerners often assume that they have agreement and resume talking before a Malaysian has the chance to respond.

Business Entertaining

- Take advantage of any invitations to social events. Establishing successful business relationships hinges on establishing strong social relationships.
- Food is vitally important in Malaysian culture. Indeed, the standard Chinese greeting literally means "Have you eaten?"
- Invitations to social events may not come immediately. Be patient and let the Malaysians make the first invitation. You cannot successfully host a social event until you have been a guest at a Malaysian event.
- Respond to written invitations in writing.
- Generally, spouses may be invited to dinners but not to lunch. However, no business will be discussed at an event where spouses are present.

Cultural Note

Among all ethnic groups, kissing in public (even a quick peck on a cheek) is considered unacceptable. Only the most fashionable and cosmopolitan of Malaysians will give even a quick kiss in greeting.

⊙ PROTOCOL

Greetings

- Malaysia has three major ethnic groups, each with its own traditions: Malay, Chinese, and Indian.
- With younger or foreign-educated Malaysians, a handshake is the most common form of greeting. The standard Malaysian handshake is more of a handclasp; it is rather gentle and lasts for some ten or twelve seconds. (By contrast, most North American handshakes last for only three or four seconds.) Often, both hands will be used.
- In Malaysia, westernized women may shake hands with both men and women. Malaysian businessmen usually wait for a woman to offer her hand. It is perfectly acceptable for a woman to simply nod upon an introduction rather than offering her hand. A woman should offer her hand only upon greetings; too-frequent handshaking is easily misinterpreted as an amorous advance. (Among themselves, men tend to shake hands both on greeting and on departure.)
- Ethnic Malays are generally Muslim. Traditionally, there is no physical contact between Muslim men and women. (Indeed, if a religious Muslim male is touched by a woman, he must ritually cleanse himself before he prays again.) Because of this, women should not offer to shake hands with Malay men, nor should men offer to shake hands with Malay women. Of course, if a westernized Malay offers to shake hands, do so.
- The traditional Malay greeting is the salaam, which is akin to a handshake without the grip. Both parties stretch out one or both hands, touch each other's hand(s) lightly, then bring their hand(s) back to rest over their heart. This greeting is done only between

people of the same sex: from man to man or from woman to woman. However, if cloth (such as a scarf or shawl) prevents actual skin-to-skin contact, then a Malay man and woman may engage in the salaam.

- Among Malaysian Chinese, the traditional greeting is a bow. However, most now shake hands or combine a bow with a handshake. Chinese men are likely to be comfortable shaking hands with a woman—more so than men from other ethnic groups of Malaysia.

- Many Malay Indians are Hindu. Most Hindus avoid public contact between men and women, although not as assiduously as observant Muslims. Men may shake hands with men and women with women, but only westernized Hindus will shake hands with the opposite sex. Malaysian Indians may also be Sikhs or Christians or Muslims; all avoid public contact between the sexes.

- The traditional Indian greeting involves a slight bow with the palms of the hands together (as if praying). This greeting, called the *namaste*, will generally be used only by older, traditional Hindus. However, it is also an acceptable alternative to a handshake when a Western businesswoman greets an Indian man.

- Just as the British greeting "How do you do?" is rhetorical, Malaysians have many rhetorical greetings. Chinese greetings often involve food. "Have you eaten?" or "Have you taken food?" are rhetorical greetings; answer "yes," even if you are hungry. Similarly, a typical Malaysian greeting when meeting on the street is "Where are you going?" This is also rhetorical; "For a walk" or "Nowhere of importance" are perfectly acceptable answers—indeed, the latter is the English equivalent of the traditional Malay response. You are not expected to reveal your itinerary.

Titles/Forms of Address

- Addressing Malaysians properly is a complex affair, especially for Westerners unfamiliar with the naming patterns of Malaysian ethnic groups. Take your time over an introduction, which will probably involve business cards. Repeat the title and name of the person and ask if you are pronouncing them correctly. This often invites an explanation of the history or origin of titles or names, providing you with personal information that may be useful.

- Malaysia is a constitutional monarchy with nine royal houses. With so many royals, international business visitors are likely to encounter one sooner or later. Titles and means of address vary; ask a native how a particular royal should be addressed.

- Never be overly familiar with a business contact. Most executives you meet should be addressed with a title and their name. If a person does not have a professional title (such as Engineer, Doctor, or Teacher), a westerner may use "Mr." or "Madam/Mrs./Miss" plus the name. However, be aware that you may be omitting other titles that are important both to the person and to your understanding of that person.

The traditional Malay forms of Mr., Mrs., or Miss are:

Mr. = *Encik (which may be abbreviated as "En")*
Mrs. or Madame = *Puan*
Miss (an unmarried woman) = *Cik*

These are used in front of an individual's name (e.g., Mr. Ahmadi would be properly addressed as Encik Ahmadi.) Although there is no Malay equivalent for "Ms.," the current trend is to use Puan for any adult female.

- There are additional titles that may be used once you become closer to your Malaysian associates. One title which is important in business circles is *Tuan*, which is conferred when a man is in a respected position of authority.

- When you ask Malaysian associates about their titles and names, explain about yours as well. They may be equally unsure as to which of your names is your surname. Follow their lead as to the degree of formality. Don't tell a Malaysian "just call me Tony" when you are calling him Dr. Gupta.

- Each of the three major ethnic groups in Malaysia has different naming patterns. For information on the proper titles and forms of address for Muslims, Indians, and Chinese, please see Appendix A.

Cultural Note

As part of the "Vision 2020" plan for Malaysia, an economic center for information technology (IT) was built, called the Multimedia Super Corridor (MSC). The MSC officially starts at the Petronas Twin Towers (which were the tallest buildings in the world until they were topped by a building in Taipei in 2004) and runs for fifty kilometers. It also includes Putrajaya—a largely commuter-based area for administrative and federal offices, and Cyberjaya, a technology center.

Gestures

- Aside from handshakes, there is no public contact between the sexes in Malaysia. Do not kiss or hug a person of the opposite sex in public—even if you are husband and wife. On the other hand, contact between people of the same sex is permitted. Men may hold hands with men or even walk with their arms around each other; this is interpreted as nothing except friendship.
- Among both Muslims and Hindus, the left hand is considered unclean. Eat with your right hand only. Where possible, do not touch anything or anyone with your left hand if you can use your right hand instead. Accept gifts and hold cash in the right hand. (Obviously, when both hands are needed, use them both.)
- The foot is also considered unclean. Do not move anything with your feet, and do not touch anything with your feet.
- Do not show the soles of your feet (or shoes). This restriction determines how one sits: You can cross your legs at the knee, but not place one ankle on your knee. However, any form of leg crossing is ostentatiously casual in Malaysia; never cross your legs in the presence of Malaysian royalty.
- Do not prop your feet up on anything not intended for feet, such as a desk.
- It is impolite to point at anyone with the forefinger. Malays use a forefinger only to point at animals. Even pointing with two fingers is impolite among many Indians. When you must indicate something or someone, use the entire right hand (palm out). You can also point with your right thumb, as long as all four fingers are curled down. (Make sure all your fingers are curled—older

Malays would interpret a fist with the thumb and little finger extended as an insult.)

- Pounding one fist into the palm of the other hand is considered obscene.
- The head is considered the seat of the soul by many Indians and Malays. Never touch someone's head, not even to pat the hair of a child.
- Among Indians, a side-to-side toss of one's head indicates agreement, although Westerners may interpret it to mean "no." Watch carefully; the Indian head toss is not quite the same as the Western negative nod (which leads with the jaw).
- As in much of the world, to beckon someone, you hold your hand out, palm downward, and make a scooping motion with the fingers. Beckoning someone with the palm up and wagging one finger, as in the USA, can be construed as an insult.
- Standing tall with your hands on your hips—the "arms akimbo" position—is always interpreted as an angry, aggressive posture.
- The comfortable standing distance between two people in Malaysia varies with each culture. In general, stand as far apart as you would if you were about to shake hands (about two to three feet). Indians tend to stand a bit further apart (three or three and a half feet).

Gifts

- The Malaysian Anti-Corruption Agency has strict laws against bribery. Avoid giving gifts that could be interpreted as bribes.
- Gifts are exchanged between friends. Do not give a gift to anyone before you have established a personal relationship with her or him. Otherwise, the gift may have the appearance of a bribe.
- It is not the custom to unwrap a gift in the presence of the giver. To do so would suggest that the recipient is greedy and impatient. Worse, if the gift is somehow inappropriate or disappointing, both parties would be embarrassed. Expect the recipient to thank you briefly, then put the still-wrapped gift aside until you have left.
- Because pork and alcohol are prohibited to observing Muslims, do not give them as gifts to Malays. Other foods make good gifts,

although meat products must be halal (the Muslim equivalent of kosher). The prohibition against pork and alcohol also precludes pigskin products and perfumes containing alcohol.

- Muslim Malays consider dogs unclean. Do not give toy dogs or gifts with pictures of dogs.
- Remember that personal gifts from a man to a woman can be misinterpreted as romantic offerings.
- Don't wrap gifts to ethnic Malays in white paper; white is associated with funerals.
- The Chinese traditionally decline a gift three times before accepting; this prevents them from appearing greedy. Continue to insist; once they accept the gift, say that you are pleased that they have done so.
- Gifts of food are always appreciated by Chinese, but avoid bringing food gifts with you to a dinner or party (unless it has been agreed upon beforehand). To bring food may imply that your host cannot provide enough. Instead, send food as a thank-you gift afterward. Candy or fruit baskets are good choices.
- For further information on Chinese gift-giving practices, see pages 14–15.
- Among Indians, the frangipani flower (used by Hawaiians to make leis) is used only for funeral wreaths.
- If you give money to an Indian, make sure it is an odd number (just the opposite of Chinese tradition). Usually this is done by adding a single dollar; for example, give $11 instead of $10.
- Observant Hindus do not eat beef or use products made from cattle. This eliminates most leather products as gifts.

Dress
- Just north of the Equator, Malaysia is hot and humid all year long. Most of the lowlands have a daytime temperature range of 75 to 95°F and humidity between 60 and 70 percent.
- Lower temperatures occur only in the mountainous areas, where businesspeople rarely venture (except for tourism). Mountain temperatures can actually dip below freezing at night.

- The monsoon season runs from September through December, but sudden showers occur all year long. Many people carry an umbrella every day.
- As a foreigner, you should dress conservatively until you are sure what degree of formality is expected. Men should wear a suit jacket and tie.
- Because of the heat and humidity, business dress in Malaysia is sometimes casual. Standard formal office wear for men is dark pants and a light-colored long-sleeved shirt and tie, without a jacket. Businessmen may also wear a short-sleeved shirt with no tie.
- Businesswomen wear light-colored long-sleeved blouses and skirts, or business suits.
- Many Malaysian men wear an open-necked batik shirt to work. This is also popular for casual wear. Jeans are acceptable for casual wear, but shorts should be avoided.
- In deference to Muslim and Hindu sensibilities, women should always wear garments that cover at least their upper arms. Skirts should be knee-length or longer.

Cultural Note

The use of electronic gadgets has become ubiquitous in Asia. Cell phones alone have changed cultural norms. One unfortunate example is that of a Malaysian football player who terminated his engagement via a text message the morning of the wedding! The bride then had to face 1,000 guests alone at their traditional Malaysian wedding feast. The incident appalled the player's Kedah State Football Association—and all his teammates, who had been invited to the wedding. Because he tarnished the game's image, the player's contract was terminated.

Philippines

Republic of the Philippines
Local short form: Pilipinas
Local long form: Republika ng Pilipinas

Cultural Note

Culturally, Filipinos are unique. Although the majority are of Malay stock, most have Hispanic surnames, are Roman Catholic (this is the only Christian nation in Asia), and speak some English. This makes the Philippines the fourth-largest English-speaking country in the world, after the United States of America, the United Kingdom, and India.

▶ WHAT'S YOUR CULTURAL IQ?

1. The Philippine archipelago is comprised of 7,107 islands. Which of these is not a large Philippine island?
   a. Java
   b. Luzon
   c. Mindanao
   ANSWER: a. Java is an island, but it is part of Indonesia.

2. TRUE or FALSE? Boogong and Balut are indigenous Philippine languages.
   ANSWER: FALSE. They are traditional delicacies. A rite of passage that will endear you to Filipinos consists of eating one of the few local dishes that foreigners are squeamish about. These include the foul-smelling shrimp paste called *bogoong*, or the boiled embryonic duck egg called *balut*.

3. Which of the following women have not served as president of the Philippines?
   a. Gloria Macapagal-Arroyo

b. Imelda Marcos

c. Corazon Aquino

ANSWER: b. Imelda Marcos was the wife of former president Ferdinand E. Marcos.

▶ TIPS ON DOING BUSINESS IN THE PHILIPPINES

- Titles are important to Filipinos—so important that many employees are rewarded with impressive-sounding titles (and little else). Address an executive by his or her title and surname, but do not expect to be able to tell much about a person's importance from the title.
- Filipinos are extremely familiar with Western business practices, but that does not mean they follow them precisely. Do not expect Filipino executives to make decisions independently of their associates and upper management. They respect authority in their organizations and will want to obtain the approval of senior management before deciding on a contract. An extensive government bureaucracy slows down action even further. Be patient.
- Kinship is everything in the Philippines. You will be accepted more rapidly if you can explain your relationship to someone the Filipinos already know. Even if the relationship is distant (i.e., you are the friend of the brother of someone they know), it will help establish you as a related, connected person.
- Groups of Filipinos do not arrange themselves in neat lines. Instead, they form a pushing, shoving crowd, with each person out for him- or herself. The only times that Filipinos have queued in neat lines was under the gun of armed soldiers (such as during the Japanese occupation army in World War II).
- There is a rather short-term orientation, so break down your projects into manageable sections. Deeply involved, long-term plans can be viewed as onerous and unrealistic.

▶ COUNTRY BACKGROUND

Demographics

Approximately 90 million Filipinos (2006 estimate) live on about 2,000 islands in the Philippines. The population of Manila, the capital

and largest city, has surpassed ten million. Around 90 percent of Filipinos are Christians, and approximately 5 percent are Muslims.

History

The Philippine Islands were inhabited before recorded human
history. To this day, one can find human cultures living there at every
level of technology. Many Filipinos live in modern, bustling Pacific
Rim cities, while others live in isolated tropical jungles. This cultural
diversity began in the tenth century A.D., when the Chinese began to
trade with Filipinos. Eventually, some Chinese stayed in the Philippines. Although ethnic Chinese represent a small percent of the Philippine population, they control about half of the nation's commerce
and banking. While many prominent Filipinos have Chinese ances-
try, there is considerable hostility toward the Chinese dominance of
business.

Arab traders introduced Islam to the Philippines in the fourteenth
century. Concentrated in the southern islands, these Muslims fiercely
resisted both Spanish and American authority. Their refusal to yield
to colonial overlords is a source of pride to many Filipinos, Muslim
and Christian alike.

The Portuguese navigator Magellan led a Spanish fleet to the Philippines in 1521 and named the islands after King Philip II of Spain.
Spaniards subsequently ruled for 350 years and brought Catholicism
to the islands, as well as the Latino attitudes and traditions that are
now a major part of the Filipino makeup. Filipino nationalism also
manifested itself under Spanish domination; for example, Filipino-
born clergy agitated for equality with the Spanish clergy in the
nineteenth century. The Spanish language and culture never became
totally dominant in the Philippines, perhaps because Spain did not
rule directly. The Philippines were overseen indirectly, via Mexico.

After the Spanish-American War, the Philippines were ceded to
the United States of America in 1898. Already fighting against their
Spanish overlords, Filipinos had no desire to be ruled by another
colonial power. The Philippine insurrection against the United States
lasted over twelve years and cost the lives of hundreds of thousands
of Filipinos. But after the war, the USA brought infrastructure

development to the country. It was in the U.S.-built public schools that English became a predominant language. Under U.S. control, the nation became the Commonwealth of the Philippines in 1935.

In 1941, the Japanese conquest of the Philippines demonstrated to Filipinos that the USA was not unbeatable. The Philippines were liberated in 1945 by Allied troops, both U.S. and Filipino. Full independence for the Philippines came on July 4, 1946.

Type of Government

The Republic of the Philippines has been an independent nation since 1946. Many Filipinos see their history as a struggle against foreign domination, first by Spain, then by the USA.

The Republic of the Philippines is a unitary republic patterned after the United States of America. The president of the Philippines is both head of state and head of the government. There are two legislative houses: the Senate and the House of Representatives.

The first Philippine Constitution dates back to 1935. After the Philippines became an independent republic, U.S. military bases were a source of contention, a constant reminder of colonial domination. Furthermore, the USA exerted tremendous influence, as when it helped to keep the corrupt dictatorship of Ferdinand Marcos in power for twenty-one years! The end of the Cold War reduced the importance of the two major U.S. bases in the Philippines, Clark Air Force Base and Subic Bay Naval Base. While the U.S. and Philippine governments were negotiating over the future of the bases, Mount Pinatubo erupted in June 1991. Buried under volcanic ash, Clark Air Force Base was rendered unusable. A new deal was negotiated to allow Subic Bay Naval Base to remain open. President Corazon Aquino agreed, but the Philippine Senate rejected it. The Philippine people themselves were split over the issue; had it been put to a referendum, the majority might have voted to allow U.S. forces to remain at Subic Bay Naval Base.

In 1992 Corazon Aquino's defense minister, Fidel Ramos, was elected president. He had a stable six-year term. Following President Ramos, a former movie star was elected in 1998—Joseph Estrada. His term in office was cut short because he was charged with taking bribes, and was impeached. After President Estrada capitulated, he was replaced by the vice president, Gloria Macapagal-Arroyo. President Arroyo won a second term in 2004.

The Philippines faces a future relatively free of foreign influences, but without the millions of dollars the U.S. military presence pumped into the economy. The country struggles with unemployment, a fluctuating economy, and a huge debt load, not to mention periodic natural disasters.

Current government data can be found at the Embassy of Philippines at *www.philippineembassy.org.*

Cultural Note

Filipinos grow up in extended families and are rarely alone. Indeed, solitude makes most Filipinos uncomfortable. A foreigner's desire for privacy is not usually understood. If you are sitting alone on a bus or in a cinema, a Filipino is likely to ignore all the empty seats and sit next to you. Such action is not about you; it is simply a cultural trait.

Language

Tagalog (Pilipino, Filipino) and English are the official languages of the Republic of the Philippines. There are eight major dialects: Tagalog, Cebuano, Ilocan, Hiligaynon or Ilonggo, Bicol, Waray, Pampango, and Pangasinense. The literacy rate is approaching 90 percent.

Ethnologue.com acknowledges 172 languages in the Philippines, 3 of which are extinct.

The Philippine View

The Philippines has no official religion, but approximately 83 percent of Filipinos consider themselves Roman Catholic. While only 9 percent of Filipinos are Protestant, their Evangelical sects are growing rapidly. There is also a Philippine Independent Church, which claims some 6 percent of the population (they were Roman Catholics, but broke with Rome). Followers of Islam are concentrated in the south.

Thanks in part to the Catholic Church's opposition to birth control, the Philippines has a very high birth rate. (Former President Estrada himself had at least ten children.)

Social scientists have found that most Filipinos have a fairly low uncertainty avoidance index. Societies that score high on this scale feel the need for creating rigid rules of behavior and extensive sets of laws to enforce them. At the opposite end of the scale, Philippine society and behavior exhibits flexibility and adaptability. The letter of the law is not strictly observed, and there are not regulations to cover every situation. This situation is probably ideal for a sprawling, geographically divided, multicultural society. But it has disadvantages for foreigners who assume that laws exist to be followed. For example, comprehensive building codes do not exist in all areas of the Philippines, and where they are present, they may not be strictly adhered to or enforced.

Curiously, this does not prevent companies from adopting extensive in-house regulations for their employees. This reflects the difficulty that a supervisor has in disciplining an employee who is probably related to several company employees (or even related to the boss). By detailing punishments for various infractions, the manager stays at a dignified distance from any necessary disciplinary action.

Great inequalities exist in the Philippines. The majority of the population is poor. But mobility (or the hope of mobility) exists. The most important influence on Filipinos is the family. Nepotism is common and is not considered to be detrimental.

Cultural Note

The enforcement of regulations is often used as a weapon among competitors. One party with government connections may be allowed to flout regulations, while competitors are strictly held to the letter of the law. It is summed up in this Philippine expression: "For my friends—everything, for my enemies—the law."

☑ Know Before You Go

The Philippines is prone to disasters. Many are natural events, such as volcanoes, floods, mudslides, earthquakes, and typhoons. But some are within human control, like boat accidents. If you are considering taking a ferry, examine it closely—if it looks unsafe or overcrowded, seek alternative transportation. Whatever your travel plans, be sure to obtain medical evacuation insurance.

To avoid the monsoon season, try to schedule your visits between September and May. Avoid major Catholic holidays as well, as many Filipinos will observe Christmas and Easter celebrations.

There is a risk of getting malaria, typhus, or cholera outside of the major urban areas. Be sure to review the inoculations that your physician or the CDC (at *www.cdc.gov*) suggests.

Illegal logging has added to the high number of disasters in the Philippines. More than half of the Philippines' forests were ravaged over the last century. This deforestation, combined with fierce tropical storms, promoted flash flooding and landslides in the eastern and northern regions. These catastrophes took at least 5,000 lives in 1991, and thousands more in the northeast in late 2004.

▶ CULTURAL ORIENTATION

Cognitive Styles: How Filipinos Organize and Process Information

Filipinos love to converse. They are generally open to information, but do not change their attitudes readily. Because most of their education is by rote, they tend to process information subjectively and associatively. They tend to become personally involved in problems rather than using rules and laws to solve them.

Negotiation Strategies: What Filipinos Accept as Evidence

Most truth comes from direct feelings. Although some absolute truths may rest on faith in ideologies (such as those of the Catholic Church), few are easily traced back to objective facts.

Value Systems: The Basis for Behavior

The culture of the Philippines is rich and diverse. China, Islam, Spain, and the United States all left their marks. The following three sections identify the Value Systems in the predominant culture—their methods of dividing right from wrong, good from evil, and so forth.

Locus of Decision-Making

Individuals act in the context of a group (the family is the most important group). Thus, they must seek the consensus of the group, because the individual rarely feels that he or she has the final say on anything. Decisions are made from a relational perspective. Filipinos must get to know you, and this involves asking about your family and personal background. Rather than presenting their own ideas, they more often react to the input of others. It is difficult for them to be confrontational and give an outright "no."

Sources of Anxiety Reduction

The nuclear and extended family is the main source of support and stability. The whole family may be shamed by the action of one member. Much of the stability of life is found in the adherence to tradition, especially the observance of rituals that maintain relationships. Many of these are connected with religion. Interpersonal relationships bring with them a sense of obligation. Reciprocity in relationships is practiced on all levels, and paying one's obligations binds the persons involved more closely.

Issues of Equality/Inequality

Filipino politics is a system that serves its players, not the people. However, Filipinos are strongly in favor of democracy, individual freedom, education, and freedom of the press. Filipinos are very status conscious. This sometimes extends to issues of race—for example, the lighter the skin, the higher the status. There is a preoccupation with chastity and safety.

▶ BUSINESS PRACTICES

Punctuality, Appointments, and Local Time

- Business hours are generally from 8:00 A.M. to 5:00 P.M., Monday through Friday.
- Offices may close for a lunch break, which can easily stretch for two hours. Some offices may open from 8:00 A.M. to 12:00 noon on Saturdays.
- Time is malleable. Foreign executives are expected to be on time to business meetings. Filipinos tend to be reasonably punctual.
- Everyone, even foreigners, is expected to be late for social events. But the exact measure of the delay depends upon the status of each

person. (The highest-ranking person should arrive last.) Rather than try to decipher the ranking of each party guest, foreigners should just ask their host (in private) what time they should actually arrive.

- The exception to the socially correct delay is the Filipino wedding. Guests are expected to arrive on time. Only the bride may be late.

- Appointments can be scheduled far in advance of your arrival in the Philippines.

- English is the language of most business transactions and virtually all business or government correspondence.

- Without introductions, it is very difficult to meet decision-makers. You will end up scheduling many appointments with subordinates. Not only will you have to progress through levels of influence, but you must progress through levels of formality—from introductions at social events, to semiofficial luncheons, to scheduled business meetings.

- A skilled representative is often hired to cut through several levels of management to get to the decision-maker.

- Midmornings, midafternoons, or late afternoons are usually best for appointments.

- The official national Independence Day holiday is June 12th, which was the date of declaration of independence from Spain (in 1898). July, 4th, 1946, was their date of independence from the United States of America. For the official holidays of the Philippines, visit *www.kissboworshakehands.com.*

- The Philippines is eight hours ahead of Greenwich Mean Time (G.M.T. + 8), or thirteen hours ahead of U.S. Eastern Standard Time (E.S.T. + 13).

Cultural Note

Filipinos are strong believers in forging relationships and maintaining *pakikisama* (smooth relations) at all costs. Confrontation is unthinkable and a sign of disrespect. Part of this process is the *utang na loob* (reciprocity) system whereby one business (or political) connection leads to other, more lucrative, deals. Acceptance of a favor or reference will call for a larger one in return. Beware the Filipino bearing gifts—a simple "thank you" will not suffice.

Negotiating

- The pace of business negotiations in the Philippines is slower than in northern Europe or North America. It would be unusual to complete a complex transaction in only one trip.
- Negotiating is generally done in a formal, precise manner. Pay attention to the hierarchy of the negotiators, and maintain a respectful, professional demeanor. The higher the negotiator's position, the more formal your interactions should be.
- Speak in quiet, gentle tones. Filipinos revere harmony. The only time you are likely to hear loud Filipinos is when they are boisterously happy.
- Filipinos want to please the people they are speaking to, so they are liable to say "yes" to offers. This simply means that the Filipinos do not want to offend you with an outright "no." In the Philippines, "yes" can mean anything from "I agree" to "maybe" to "I hope you can tell from my lack of enthusiasm that I really mean 'no.'"
- To ensure that a Filipino really means yes, you must get it in writing. If possible, try to get written agreement at each stage in your negotiations. Filipinos feel honor-bound to fulfill a written commitment.
- Expect to see your Filipino business partners often at social situations. Never decline an invitation to a social event.
- When you interrupt Filipinos during a meal, they are obliged to ask you to join in. This is a formality; just thank them and decline, saying that you have already eaten.
- Remember that social contacts are more important in the Philippines than business ones. A Filipino must like you and be comfortable with you in order to do business. This relationship does not extend to your company. If your company replaces you with another executive, the new executive will have to forge this relationship anew (unless the new executive is a blood relative of yours).
- Business cards may be printed in English; it is not necessary to translate them into Pilipino. The exchange of business cards is more casual than in other parts of Asia; a Filipino businessperson to whom you have given a card may—or may not—give you one

of his or hers. The visiting businessperson should be the first to offer a card.

- If a Filipino gives you a business card with their home phone handwritten upon it, take that as an invitation to call. Business in the Philippines evolves out of social interaction, most of which takes place outside the office.

- Once you are accepted, Filipinos are very sociable and love to talk. Expect to be asked very personal questions, such as "Why are you not married?" They will also ask how much you paid for something, out of concern that you may have been cheated.

Cultural Note

Filipinos smile constantly. However, as with the Japanese, a smile is not a ubiquitous sign of pleasure, affection, or amusement.

Filipinos may smile or laugh in situations that Westerners consider inappropriate. Smiles hide embarrassment and discord. Filipino businessmen may laugh at the most serious part of a business meeting, and a Filipino physician may smile while telling a patient he is seriously ill.

While foreigners are not expected to smile as much as Filipinos, they are expected to restrain their tempers. As in other parts of Asia, it is considered shameful to express anger in public; a person who loses his or her temper is not respected.

Furthermore, because the Philippines is a more violent country than Japan, Thailand, etc., expressing anger at someone can easily provoke a similar response. Foreigners can unintentionally push a Filipino into a public outburst, as the Filipino feels he must act to regain his honor—whatever the cost. If you must reprimand a Filipino employee, do it calmly and in private.

Business Entertaining

- Food is vitally important in Filipino culture. Social occasions always involve food. In reality, the standard Pilipino greeting *"Kumain ka na ba?"* translates as "Have you eaten?"

- Celebrate the conclusion of a business deal by inviting your Filipino partners to a restaurant. The person who issued the invitation always pays—unless it was a woman, in which case most Filipino businessmen will insist upon paying.

- Invite the wives of your business partners to dinner, but not to a luncheon. Expect to be invited to dinners and parties at the home of your Filipino partner (unless he or she is Chinese; Chinese rarely entertain at home). Such parties traditionally have numerous guests, including many relatives. Remember to show respect for elders. You may or may not be individually introduced to everyone.
- Most households have servants, including a cook. Compliment the hostess on the decor, but be aware that she probably did not prepare the food herself.
- Desserts are very popular in the Philippines at both lunch and dinner. If you are hosting a luncheon, be sure to provide a dessert.
- Social events often end with dancing and singing. Expect to be invited to sing.
- Despite boisterous partying and hard drinking (by men), Filipinos find public drunkenness shameful. Do not get out of control.

Cultural Note

Never appear too eager to begin eating at a party; allow the hostess to ask you several times to sit down. A person who jumps at food is considered uncouth and greedy.

This behavior holds true for social invitations also. Invitations must be extended multiple times, and Filipinos will probably respond with a polite "yes" without feeling committed to attend. Reconfirm the invitation at least once. Do not be surprised if someone declines via a third party. You can try sending out written invitations with an RSVP, but because Filipinos feel honor-bound by written commitments, few will respond.

⊛ PROTOCOL

Greetings

- Foreign businessmen should expect to shake hands firmly with Filipino men, both upon introduction and at subsequent meetings.
- Traditionally, there is no physical contact between men and women in public. Men should wait for a Filipino woman to offer her hand, which most Filipino businesswomen will do.

- Foreign businesswomen may initiate a handshake with Filipino men or women.
- Close female friends in the Philippines hug and kiss upon greeting. Similarly, close male friends may exhibit extended physical contact, such as holding hands or leaving an arm around a friend's shoulder.

Cultural Note

Many Filipinos did not have surnames until the mid-nineteenth century. In 1849, the Spanish governor ordered all Filipinos to adopt Hispanic surnames. Families chose surnames from lists provided by the government, and the first letter of every surname on a list was specific to a particular area. Thus, people from one town or area all had surnames beginning with the letter *A*, the next town used *B*, and so on. Even today, the first letter of a person's surname can provide information about where his or her family originally came from.

Titles/Forms of Address

- Most people you meet should be addressed with a title and their surname. Many professionals have titles, because Filipino companies may reward employees with titles instead of additional pay or responsibilities.
- Persons who do not have professional titles should be addressed, in English, as "Mr.," "Mrs.," or "Miss," plus their surname.
- Wives of persons with important titles are sometimes addressed as "Mrs." plus the husband's title (e.g., Mrs. Senator or Mrs. Mayor).
- Upper-class Filipinos may follow the Hispanic tradition of having two surnames: one from their father, which is listed first, followed by one from their mother.
- Most Filipinos have nicknames, many of which sound incongruous to foreigners. Once a Filipino invites you to address him or her by a nickname, you are expected to do so. An example is the recent vice president of the Philippines, Manuel de Castro, who went by "Noli."
- After such an invitation, you should invite a Filipino to address you by your nickname. (If you don't have one, you might like to make one up).

- Flattery by means of "verbal promotion" is common in the Philippines. A police officer may be referred to as "Captain," a police captain may be called "Major," and so on.

Gestures

- A great deal of information can be communicated via eye contact and eyebrow movement. Filipinos may greet each other by making eye contact followed by raising and lowering the eyebrows.
- A traditional Filipino may demonstrate respect upon greeting an elder by placing the elder's hand or knuckles on his or her forehead.
- Because of the years of U.S. military presence in the Philippines, most North American gestures are recognized.
- The foremost obscene gesture in both the USA and the Philippines involves an extended middle finger. However, in the Philippines, that finger is pointed at the person or thing being insulted.
- Since pointing can easily be taken for an insulting gesture, Filipinos rarely indicate objects or directions by pointing with their fingers. Instead, they indicate with a glance or by pursing their lips.
- Indicating "two" with the fingers is done by holding up the ring and little finger, instead of the forefinger and middle finger. The thumb is not used to count numbers in the Philippines.
- Staring has various nuances in the Philippines, most of them negative. Foreigners should avoid staring at Filipinos, who can easily interpret a stare as belligerence. If you are stared at, look away.
- As in much of the world, to beckon someone you hold your hand out, palm downward, and make a scooping motion with the fingers. Beckoning someone with the palm up and wagging one finger, as in the USA, can be construed as an insult.
- To stand tall with your hands on your hips—the "arms akimbo" or "offsides" position in soccer—is always interpreted as an aggressive posture. Worse, it expresses an aggressive challenge—and in the Philippines, belligerence is often met with belligerence.
- Looking down is useful to avoid giving offense when making one's way through a crowd or between two people who are conversing.

This may also be accompanied by an outstretched, flat hand (like a karate chop) or with both hands clasped together; the hand(s) are in front, preceding the direction of motion.

- A Filipino may try to attract your attention by brushing a finger against your elbow.

Gifts

- Gift giving is an important part of Filipino society. Flowers and food are the most common gifts, although there are situations in which a handful of small coins is traditional.
- When invited to a Filipino home, bring (or have sent before you arrive) flowers or a delicacy to your hostess. Avoid bringing alcohol or a substantial food, as this may imply that your host cannot serve enough to satisfy guests.
- However, exceptions are made for a specialty dish or food that only you can provide, such as a recipe from your home country. A thank-you note is appropriate afterward; some people also send a small gift.
- After a dinner party, Filipinos often give their guests extra food to take home, an ancient tradition called *pabaon*.
- At Christmas, you will be expected to give a token gift—such as a company calendar—to seemingly everyone you know or do business with. Your list should include everyone who works for you, all service personnel you deal with regularly (your postal clerks, your security guards), and anyone who makes your life easier by cooperating with you, such as the secretary of an important client.
- Filipinos follow the Asian habit of not opening gifts in the presence of the giver. Traditionally, if the recipient is not happy with the gift, he or she avoids embarrassment by opening it away from the giver. Furthermore, Filipinos abhor appearing greedy; to open a gift immediately would give this impression. Do not be dismayed if your gift is casually set aside and ignored; you will be thanked for it at a later date.
- For further suggestions on appropriate gifts in the Philippines, visit *www.kissboworshakehands.com*.

Dress

- Because of the heat and humidity, business dress for Filipinos is often casual: dark trousers and white, short-sleeved shirts for men, without a tie; white long-sleeved blouses and skirts or pantsuits for women. Despite this simplicity, these clothes will be neat, clean, and fashionable. Filipinos are very style conscious.
- You should dress conservatively until you are sure what degree of formality is expected. Men should wear a suit and tie; businesswomen wear white blouses and dark suits, pantsuits, or skirts.
- Many Filipino men wear an embroidered shirt called a *barong tagalog*. It is worn without a tie and hangs outside the trousers, untucked. Long-sleeved ones are often worn to work and to semiformal occasions; short-sleeved ones are for casualwear.
- Men may wear a business suit for formal occasions, such as the theater, a formal dinner party, and so forth, but women are expected to wear a cocktail dress. Long evening gowns are required only on rare occasions, such as diplomatic functions.
- Neither men nor women should wear shorts or sandals in public, except at the beach. Because Filipinos are so competitively fashionable, some offices require their workers to wear uniforms.
- Don't wear anything outside that can be damaged by water during a fiesta. Drenching pedestrians is a favorite fiesta pastime.

Singapore

Republic of Singapore

Cultural Note

Singapore remains a booming center of capitalism in Southeast Asia. It is considered exceptionally safe (even antiseptic), however, visitors should remember that Singapore's myriad laws apply to natives and foreigners equally. Before arrival, travelers should become familiar with these laws: for example, no littering, no non-prescription chewing gum, no illegal drugs, no pornographic materials, no weapons, no jaywalking, no spitting, and no smoking in most public places. There is speculation that some of these stringent laws will ease in the future, but to date, they are unfailingly enforced.

▶ WHAT'S YOUR CULTURAL IQ?

1. Which of the following is true about driving in Singapore?
   a. Singapore enforces traffic regulations with cameras that monitor violations.
   b. Many Singaporeans drivers are unpredictable on the road.
   c. A branch with green leaves adorning a stopped car indicates that the vehicle has broken down.
   d. Cars are driven on the left side of the road.
   e. All of the above are true.
   ANSWER: e. Traffic is a combination of high-tech (cameras), tradition (a branch stuck in the bumper of a broken-down car), and temperaments.

2. The government of Singapore applies its draconian legal code to citizens and visitors alike. TRUE or FALSE: Singapore is one of the few nations that still sentences criminals to be caned.
   ANSWER: TRUE. In fact, a teenager named Michael Fay (a U.S. citizen) was caned for vandalism in 1994, despite the intercession of then-U.S. president Bill Clinton.

3. After Sir Stamford Raffles established a trading post on Singapore Island in 1819, it was ruled by the United Kingdom for over a century. TRUE or FALSE: Singapore briefly joined with newly independent Indonesia in 1963.
   ANSWER: FALSE. Singapore joined the Federation of Malaysia in 1963. In 1965, Singapore left and became independent.

▶ TIPS ON DOING BUSINESS IN SINGAPORE

- All of the ethnic groups in Singapore prefer intermittent eye contact. This is especially true in situations between persons of unequal station: the person with lower status does not meet the gaze of his or her superior. Westerners sometimes interpret this failure to "look me in the eye" as evidence of untrustworthiness. On the contrary, in Singapore, sustained eye contact is considered hostile and threatening.

- One reason for the government's tight control over Singapore's populace is that it is a multicultural society. Singapore's ethnic Chinese dominate the business sector, just as they do in nearby Malaysia and Indonesia. Traditionally, this generated resentment on the part of the Indian population and the native ethnic Malays. The government has multiple programs to foster national unity.

- English is widely spoken in Singapore. It is one of the country's four official languages, and is the standard language for international business. Even the government writes its official correspondence in English.

- The word "no" is rarely heard. You are more likely to hear a polite but evasive "yes." In Singapore, the response "yes" can mean anything from "I agree" to "I hope you can tell from my lack of enthusiasm that I really mean 'no.'" Listen for this clue; whenever there are any qualifications attached, it probably means no.

- Offer your most advanced technical proposals in Singapore. It is a country where they are aggressive about innovative training in their schools and technology in their industries. Determined not to be left behind in the high-tech arena, Singapore is striving to become a center for stem-cell research.

▶ COUNTRY BACKGROUND

Demographics
About 4,500,000 people live in this tiny nation (2006 estimate). As a prosperous trading center, Singapore attracts many races. The indigenous Malay now constitute approximately 15 percent of Singapore's citizenry. Numerous ethnic groups from the Indian subcontinent call Singapore home; together they make up about 7 percent of the population of Singapore. The vast majority (76 percent) of Singaporeans are Chinese. Europeans now constitute less than 1 percent of Singapore's population.

History
A crossroads of trade for centuries, Singapore was annexed by the British in 1819. British rule was to last some 120 years, and gave the island British legal traditions and the English language. During World War II, the Japanese occupied Singapore from 1942 to 1945. After the war Singapore became a British crown colony, but the power of the British Empire was fading.

Singapore's first election was held in 1959. The People's Action Party (PAP) took the election and has remained in power ever since. The first prime minister was Cambridge-educated Lee Kuan Yew. Singapore experienced tremendous development under Lee and the PAP.

Singapore joined the Malayan Federation in 1963, but it seceded just two years later. Since 1965 it has been a separate, sovereign nation and a member of the British Commonwealth.

Many did not believe that Singapore could survive as an independent country. The tiny island had no natural resources aside from its harbor, and no way to defend itself against populous and often aggressive neighbors. Realizing that Singapore's people were its greatest national asset, Prime Minister Lee Kuan Yew's government embarked upon social engineering on a grand scale. The people would be educated, and capitalism would be encouraged. Old traditions were suppressed, and Singapore was turned into a true meritocracy.

No aspect of life was considered beyond the reach of the government. The "3-S Plan" of Social Responsibility, Social Attitude, and Skill became an official credo. Citizens were constantly reminded of the threat from Singapore's populous neighbors, and internal dissent was silenced. Tiny Singapore built up defense forces with the most up-to-date technology in the world. However, opponents of the government were sometimes jailed without trial; overly critical foreign journalists were deported, and any publication that employed such a journalist was liable to be banned from sale in Singapore.

Thankfully, Singapore was spared serious damage in the disastrous Boxing Day tsunami of 2004. Singapore has also made progress in its various long-term disputes with neighboring Malaysia.

Type of Government

The Republic of Singapore is a parliamentary democracy that has been ruled by one party since the nation achieved independence from Malaysia in 1965. The government exhorts its people to accept stringent limitations on freedom in return for peace and prosperity. These limitations often make Singapore more attractive from a business standpoint. (For example, Singapore's citizens have a high rate of savings, because participation in the Central Provident Fund—a pension program—is mandatory for all citizens.)

The leaders of Singapore are fond of saying that their island's only resources are the wit, industry, and inventiveness of the Singaporean people. They have successfully turned a developing nation into a center of capitalism.

Singapore has a unicameral parliament. The prime minister is the head of government. The chief of state is the president.

Current government data can be found at the Embassy of Singapore at *www.mfa.gov.sg/washington*.

Cultural Note

Although English is commonly spoken, it is a unique version. Singaporeans tend to imprint English with the patterns of their native tongue. There is even a term for this Singapore-English: Singlish.

Language

Singapore has four official languages: Malay, Tamil, Chinese, and English. To unify Singapore's three fractious ethnic groups—the Chinese, Malays, and Indians—English (native to none of these groups) became the language of instruction, business, and government. (This process has not ended; to unify the diverse Chinese populations, only Mandarin Chinese movies may be shown—despite the fact that most Singaporean Chinese speak Cantonese, not Mandarin.) Both Malay and English are printed using the Latin alphabet; Tamil and Chinese use their traditional forms of writing.

For data on the various languages of Singapore, see Ethnologue at *www.ethnologue.com.*

Cultural Note

Islam conquered much of the Middle East and Africa by the sword. In the islands of Southeast Asia, however, Muslim traders from the Indian subcontinent brought it peacefully. Some believe that this historical distinction yields a gentler, less rigorous type of Islam. Others disagree. And it may no longer matter, as fiery fundamentalist mullahs have come to Singapore, Malaysia, and Indonesia to agitate the Muslim populace. The authorities in Singapore try to keep out such individuals, but they can't totally halt the distribution of fundamentalist literature.

The Singaporean View

Most indigenous Malays are Muslim, but not all Muslims are Malay. Muslims account for over 15 percent of the population. Similarly, Christianity is adhered to by several different ethnic groups. Those Singaporeans who trace their roots to the Indian subcontinent come from many different ethnic groups; they may be Hindu, Muslim, Christian, Zoroastrian, Sikh, or adherents of yet another religion. The majority Chinese may profess to follow Buddhism, Confucianism, Taoism, none of these, or several of the above simultaneously.

☑ Know Before You Go

Singapore is a very safe nation, where visitors are most at risk from the hot and humid weather. Although rarely seen outside garden areas, Singapore does have some dangerous wildlife, including poisonous snakes, spiders, and centipedes.

⊙ CULTURAL ORIENTATION

Cognitive Styles: How Singaporeans Organize and Process Information

Singapore's culture is closed to all but select information. Singaporeans' basic education teaches them to think associatively, but higher education brings in conceptual and analytical thinking. They have strong loyalties to their nation, companies, and groups, but particular relationships are more important than personal values.

Negotiation Strategies: What Singaporeans Accept as Evidence

Immediate feelings have a strong influence on the truth. This is usually biased by faith in the ideologies of nationalism, and supplemented by the accumulation of objective facts.

Value Systems: The Basis for Behavior

The strong Malay and Indian subcultures have different value systems from those of the Chinese. The following three sections identify the Value Systems in the predominant culture—their methods of dividing right from wrong, good from evil, and so forth.

Locus of Decision-Making

Individuals must work within the consensus of the group and forgo personal triumphs. The person with the highest ethos in the group (usually the oldest member) is the de facto leader. One must not lose face or cause another to be publicly embarrassed, so Singaporeans would rather use polite vagaries than utter an outright "no." There is a very strong authoritative structure that demands impartiality and obedience. One must build a relationship with the participants of a group before conducting business.

Sources of Anxiety Reduction

The family is the most important unit of social organization. Political power, wealth, and education are the criteria for social status. There is a very strong work ethic in which emotional restraint is prized and aggressive behavior is frowned upon. Although this is a multiracial society with strong national identity, the social structure continues to change, and this leads to uncertainty. Multiracial housing has fostered feelings of insecurity, not community.

Issues of Equality/Inequality

Businesses are more competitive and ethnocentric than in the USA. Emphasis is on competence, merit, and team play. Performance, progress, excellence, and achievement are highly prized for the group. There is an inherent trust in people of the same ethnic group, with a strong feeling of interdependency among members of a group or business. There is some evidence of ethnic bias among the dominant Chinese against the Malays and the Indians. There are clearly differentiated sex roles in society, but gender equality is creeping in. Men still dominate in most public situations.

Cultural Note

In Singapore, social events can involve different rules for different cultural groups. In general, most Singaporeans arrive on time or slightly late. Traditionalists are concerned that arriving on time to a dinner may make them appear greedy and impatient.

Once a close friendship has been established, guests may arrive a few minutes early to a social occasion. If you are the host and your guests are close friends, it is important to be ready early.

▶ BUSINESS PRACTICES

Punctuality, Appointments, and Local Time

- Business hours are generally 9:00 A.M. to 5:00 P.M., Monday through Friday. However, many offices stagger their work hours, with workers arriving any time from 7:30 A.M. to 9:30 A.M. Some offices will be open for a half day on Saturdays, generally in the morning.
- Always be on time for all business appointments. Making a Singaporean executive wait is insulting and impolite.
- Try to schedule appointments at least two weeks in advance. Executives travel frequently—especially to conferences in their area of specialization.

- English is the language of virtually all business or government correspondence, and most transactions in Singapore. However, the English spoken often has native inflections, syntax, and grammar, which can easily lead to misunderstandings.
- Remember that Singapore is a meritocracy. Few people get ahead, either in business or in government, without hard work and long hours. Executives will often work far longer days than their subordinates.
- Singaporeans write the day first, then the month, then the year (e.g., December 3, 2010, is written 3.12.10 or 3/12/10).
- For a list of the official holidays of Singapore, visit *www.kissbowor shakehands.com.*
- Singapore is eight hours ahead of Greenwich Mean Time (G.M.T. + 8), making it thirteen hours ahead of U.S. Eastern Standard Time (E.S.T. + 13).

Negotiating
- The pace of business negotiations in Singapore may be slow compared to the West. Be patient.
- It would be unusual to complete a complicated business deal in only one trip. Expect to take several trips over a period of months.
- Because polite Singaporeans rarely disagree openly, evasion, or even pretending that a question was never asked, is indicative of a "no."
- Remember that a Singaporean must like and be comfortable with you personally in order to do business. This relationship does not extend to your company. If your company replaces you with another executive, the new person will have to forge this relationship anew (unless the new executive is a blood relative of yours).
- Unwavering civility is the single most important attribute for successful relationships in Singapore. However, diplomacy in no way hinders the determination of Singaporean businesspeople to get their own way.
- People in Singapore may smile or laugh in situations that Westerners consider inappropriate. Smiles may hide embarrassment,

shyness, bitterness, and/or discord. Singaporean businessmen may laugh at the most serious part of a business meeting; this may be an expression of anxiety, not frivolity.

- In Singapore, a person who loses his or her temper in public is considered unable to control himself or herself, and will not be trusted or respected.

- Be cautious in asking Singaporean Chinese a question. English speakers would give a negative answer to the question "Isn't my order ready yet?" by responding "no" (meaning, "No, it's not ready"). The Chinese pattern is the opposite: "yes" (meaning, "Yes, it is not ready").

- Age and seniority are highly respected. If you are part of a delegation, line up so that the most important persons will be introduced first. If you are introducing two people, state the name of the most important person first (e.g., "President Smith, this is Engineer Wong").

- Speak in quiet, gentle tones. Always remain calm. Leave plenty of time for someone to respond to a statement you make; people in Singapore do not jump on the end of someone else's sentences. Politeness demands that they leave a respectful pause (as long as ten to fifteen seconds) before responding. Westerners often assume that they have agreement and resume talking before a Singaporean has a chance to respond.

- Business cards should be printed (preferably embossed) in English. Because ethnic Chinese constitute the majority of Singaporeans (and an even higher percentage of businesspeople), it is a good idea to have the reverse side of your card translated into Chinese (gold ink is the most prestigious color for Chinese characters).

- The exchange of business cards is a formal ceremony. After introductions are made, the visiting businessperson should offer his or her card. Make sure you give a card to each person present. With both hands on your card, present it to the recipient with the print facing him or her, so that he or she can read it. The recipient may receive the card with both hands, then study it for a few moments before carefully putting it away in a pocket. You should do the same when a card is presented to you. Never put a card in your back pocket, where many men carry their wallets. Do not write on someone's business card.

- Topics to avoid in conversation include any criticism of Singaporean ways, religion, bureaucracy, or politics. Also avoid any discussion of sex.
- Good topics for discussion include tourism, travel, plans for the future, organizational success (talking about personal success is considered impolite boasting), and food (while remaining complimentary to the local cuisine).

Business Entertaining

- Take advantage of any invitations to social events; successful business relationships hinge on strong social relationships.
- Food is vitally important in Singapore culture. Indeed, the standard Chinese greeting literally means "Have you eaten?"
- Respond to written invitations in writing. Among the Chinese, white and blue are colors associated with sadness; do not print invitations on paper of these colors. Red or pink paper is a good choice for invitations.
- Generally, spouses may be invited to dinners but not to lunch. However, no business will be discussed at an event where spouses are present.
- Singapore's anticorruption laws are so strict that government officials may be prohibited from attending social events.

Cultural Note

Cleanliness and order is strictly enforced. Trash collection occurs seven days a week and there are heavy fines for littering. Even the harbor is refuse-free and generally devoid of oil slicks.

⊙ PROTOCOL

Greetings

- With younger or foreign-educated Singaporeans, a handshake is the most common form of greeting. The standard Asian handshake is more of a handclasp; it is rather gentle and lasts for some ten or twelve seconds. (By contrast, most North American handshakes are very firm but last for only three or four seconds.) Often, both hands will be used.

- Singapore has three major ethnic groups, each with its own traditions: Chinese, Malay, and Indian.

- In Singapore, westernized women may shake hands with both men and women. Singaporean men usually wait for a woman to offer her hand. It is perfectly acceptable for a woman to simply nod upon an introduction rather than offer her hand. Women should offer their hands only upon greetings; too-frequent handshaking is easily misinterpreted as an amorous advance. (Among themselves, men tend to shake hands on both greeting and departure.)

- Among Singaporean Chinese, the traditional greeting was a bow. However, most now shake hands or combine a bow with a handshake. Chinese men are likely to be comfortable shaking hands with a woman—more so than other ethnic groups of Singapore.

- Singaporean Malay are generally Muslim. Traditionally, there is no physical contact between Muslim men and women. Indeed, if a religious Muslim male is touched by a woman, he must ritually cleanse himself before he prays again. Because of this, women should be careful about offering to shake hands with Malay men, and men should not offer to shake hands with Malay women. Of course, if a westernized Malay offers to shake hands, do so.

- The traditional Malay greeting is the salaam, which is akin to a handshake without the grip. Both parties stretch out one or both hands, touch each other's hand(s) lightly, then bring their hand(s) back to rest over their heart. This greeting is done only between people of the same sex. However, if cloth such as a scarf or shawl prevents actual skin-to-skin contact, then Malay men and women may engage in the salaam.

- Many, but not all, Singaporean Indians are Hindu. They avoid public contact between men and women, although not as vehemently as most Muslims. Men may shake hands with men, and women with women, but only westernized Hindus will shake hands with the opposite sex.

- The traditional Indian greeting involves a slight bow with the palms of the hands together (as if praying). This greeting, called the *namaste*, will generally be used only by older, traditional Hindus. However, it is also an acceptable alternative to a handshake when a Western businesswoman greets an Indian man.

Titles/Forms of Address
- Most people you meet should be addressed with a title and their name. If a person does not have a professional title (President, Engineer, Doctor), simply use "Mr." or "Madam," "Mrs.," or "Miss," plus their name.
- Each of the three major ethnic groups in Singapore has different naming patterns. For further information on the proper titles and forms of address in Chinese, Muslim, and Indian cultures, please consult Appendix A.
- With so many complexities, it is best to ask a Singaporean what you should call him or her. Repeat it to confirm your pronunciation is correct. Clearly explain your name and choose the same degree of formality. Don't tell a Singaporean "just call me Tony" when you are calling him Dr. Gupta.

Gestures
- Among both Muslims and Hindus, the left hand is considered unclean. Eat with your right hand only. Do not touch anything or anyone with your left hand if you can use your right hand instead. Accept gifts and hold cash in the right hand. (Obviously, when both hands are needed, use them both.)
- The foot is also considered unclean. Do not move or touch anything with your feet.
- Do not show the soles of your feet or shoes. This restriction determines how one sits: You can cross your legs at the knee, but you probably do not want to sit with one ankle on the other knee. Also, do not prop your feet up on anything not intended for feet, such as a desk.
- It is impolite to point at anyone with the forefinger. Malays use a forefinger only to point at animals. Even pointing with two

fingers is impolite among many Indians. When you must indicate something or someone, use the entire right hand (palm out). You can also point with your right thumb, as long as all four fingers are curled down. (Make sure all your fingers are curled—older Malays would interpret a fist with the thumb and little finger extended as an insult.)

- Aside from handshakes, there is no public contact between the sexes in Singapore. Do not kiss or hug a person of the opposite sex in public—even if you are husband and wife. On the other hand, contact is permitted between people of the same sex. Men may hold hands with men or even walk with their arms around each other; this is interpreted as nothing except friendship.

- Avoid pounding one fist into the palm of your other hand. It is considered an obscene gesture.

- The head is considered the seat of the soul by many Indians and Malays. Never touch someone's head, not even to pat a child.

- Among Indians, a side-to-side toss of one's head indicates agreement, although Westerners may interpret it as meaning "no." Watch carefully; the Indian head toss is not quite the same as the Western negative nod (which leads with the jaw).

- As in much of the world, to beckon someone, you hold your hand out, palm downward, and make a scooping motion with the fingers. Beckoning someone with the palm up and wagging one finger can be construed as an insult.

- Standing tall with your hands on your hips—the "arms akimbo" position (or "offsides" in soccer)—is always interpreted as an angry, aggressive posture.

- The comfortable standing distance between two people in Singapore varies with the culture. In general, stand as far apart as you would if you were about to shake hands (about 2 to 3 feet). Indians tend to stand a bit further apart (3 or 3½ feet).

Gifts
- Singapore prides itself on being the most corruption-free country in Asia. Consequently, it has strict laws against bribery. Government employees may not accept any gift at all.

- Gifts are given between friends. Do not give a gift to anyone before you have established a personal relationship with that person. Otherwise, the gift may have the appearance of a bribe.
- It is not the custom to unwrap a gift in the presence of the giver. To do so would suggest that the recipient is greedy and impatient. Worse, if the gift is somehow inappropriate or disappointing, both the recipient and the giver would be embarrassed. Expect the recipient to thank you briefly, then put the still-wrapped gift aside until you have left.
- The Chinese traditionally decline a gift three times before accepting; this prevents them from appearing greedy. Continue to insist; once they accept the gift, thank them profusely.
- Gifts of food are always appreciated by Chinese, but avoid bringing food to a dinner because it may imply that your host cannot provide enough for all. Instead, send food as a thank-you gift afterward. Candy or fruit baskets are good choices.
- Older Chinese may associate all of the following with funerals—do not give them as gifts:
  - Straw sandals
  - Clocks
  - A stork or crane (although the Western association of storks with births is known to many young Chinese)
  - Handkerchiefs (they symbolize sadness and weeping)
  - Gifts or wrapping paper where the predominant color is white, black, or blue
- Also avoid any gifts of knives, scissors, or cutting tools; to the Chinese, they suggest the severing of a friendship.
- Although the Chinese only historically brought flowers to the sick or to funerals, Western advertising has popularized flowers as gifts. Make sure you give an even number of flowers; an odd number would be very unlucky.
- At Chinese New Year, it is customary to give a gift of money in a red envelope to children and to the nongovernmental service personnel you deal with regularly. This is called a *hong bao*. Give only new bills in even numbers and even amounts. Many employers give each employee a hong bao equal to one month's salary.

- As pork and alcohol are prohibited to observing Muslims, do not give them as gifts to Malays. Other foods make good gifts, although meat products must be halal (the Muslim equivalent of kosher). The prohibition against pork and alcohol also precludes pigskin products and perfumes containing alcohol.
- Malays consider dogs unclean. Do not give toy dogs or gifts that picture dogs.
- Should you give money to an Indian, make sure it is an odd number (just the opposite of Chinese tradition). Usually this is done by adding a single dollar; for example, give $11 instead of $10.
- Observant Hindus do not eat beef or use cattle products. This eliminates most leather products as gifts.

Dress
- Singapore is only some 85 miles (136.8 km) north of the Equator. It is hot and humid all year long, with a temperature ranging between 75 and 88°F (24 to 31°C), and humidity above 90 percent.
- The rainy season is November through January, but sudden showers occur all year long. Some people carry an umbrella every day.
- As a foreigner, you should dress more conservatively until you know what degree of formality is expected. Men should be prepared to wear a suit jacket, but can remove it if it seems appropriate.
- Because of the heat and humidity, business dress in Singapore is often casual. Standard formal office wear for men is dark trousers, light-colored long-sleeved shirts, and ties, without jackets. Some businessmen wear a short-sleeved shirt with no tie.
- Businesswomen may wear business suits and/or pantsuits. Fashions for businesswomen tend to be more frilly and decorative than those worn by Western businesswomen.
- Some Singaporean men may wear an open-necked batik shirt to work. These are also popular for casual wear. Jeans are good for casual situations, but shorts should be avoided.
- In deference to Muslim and Hindu sensibilities, women should always wear blouses that cover at least their upper arms. Skirts should be knee length or longer.

South Korea

Republic of Korea
Local long form: Taehan-min'guk
Note: the South Koreans generally use the term *Han'guk* to refer to their country
Abbreviation: ROK

Cultural Note

While there are many religions in Korea, Confucianism exerts the strongest influence on society. It is not a religion centered around the worship of a supreme deity, but rather a rigid ethical and moral system that governs all relationships. It was established by Confucius, a Chinese scholar and statesman who lived during Chinese feudal times over 2,000 years ago.

▶ WHAT'S YOUR CULTURAL IQ?

1. Which of the following games are the most popular in Korea?
   a. Chess
   b. *Changgi* (also called "Janggi")
   c. *Go* (also called "Baduk")
   ANSWER: c. Go is so popular, there are Korean television channels dedicated solely to its broadcast in South Korea. Koreans have won the $400,000 "Ing Cup" since its inception, and clearly believe in the Chinese proverb—chess is a battle, but go is war. (Janggi is a variant of chess.)

2. TRUE or FALSE? There are less than 300 family names in Korea.
   ANSWER: TRUE. Some of the most common are Kim (meaning gold) Lee (meaning plum) and Park (which means gourd).

3. Confucianism is a belief system, which contains five constant superior/subordinate relationships that must be maintained. TRUE or FALSE? They are: ruler and subject, parent and child,

elder and younger brother, husband and wife, elder friend and
younger friend.

ANSWER: TRUE. Confucianism also mandates *Jen* (a sense of duty to humanity), *Shu*
(reciprocity—"Do unto others as you would have them do unto you," similar to the Gospel of
Matthew 7:12), *Chih* (wisdom), *Wen* (representing all the arts), and respect for the *Chun tzu*
(the civilized man who has developed all the virtues).

▶ TIPS ON DOING BUSINESS IN SOUTH KOREA

- Koreans are more independent and individualistic than their
  Asian neighbors. They are the most straightforward of all Asians
  but can also be defensive, a trait stemming from a history of invasion by their neighbors.
- Seers are often consulted by Koreans in all walks of life. Even
  executives confer with them about business transactions. A negative report from a seer, or fortuneteller, could ruin an entire deal.
  A fortuneteller is called a *mudang* in Korean.
- Bad news is never given to a manager at the start of the day.
- Foreigners should attempt to show proper respect to Korean
  supervisors. This includes not putting anything on the manager's
  desk (not even sales literature) during a presentation. Korean
  executives are very territorial about their desks.
- Koreans do not maintain as much eye contact as North Americans.
  As a general rule, Koreans of equal status will look at each other
  only half of the time during their conversation. When persons are
  of unequal status, the lower-ranking person will often avert his or
  her eyes during much of the conversation. Extended or intense
  eye contact can be associated with anger. North Americans who
  try to maintain continuous eye contact with a Korean may appear
  hostile or aggressive.

▶ COUNTRY BACKGROUND

Demographics
South Korea's population of 49 million (2006 estimate) is ethnically
homogeneous (99.9 percent Korean with a small Chinese minority).

History

Korea's original name, *Choson*, meant "land of the morning calm." The country's history has been shaped by frequent invasions from its neighbors. Korean history is divided into three main periods: the Silla (668–935), Koryo (935–1392), and Yi (1392–1910) dynasties. The name "Korea" is derived from the middle dynasty of Koryo. Foreign influence—direct and indirect—occurred throughout these dynasties. All of Korea's foreign overlords—Mongolian, Chinese, and Japanese—instituted a closed-door policy in order to solidify their rule. This isolation earned Korea the name of the Hermit Kingdom.

In 1910, Japan annexed Korea and enforced ruthless control, outlawing Korean culture and language. Despite resistance, several generations grew up more familiar with Japanese than with Korean customs. At the Yalta Conference at the end of World War II, the United States of America and the Soviet Union jointly established temporary administrative trusteeship over Korea until democratic elections could be held. Japanese forces south of the thirty-eighth parallel surrendered to the USA and forces in the north surrendered to the USSR. The Soviets blocked attempts to hold nationwide elections, and the two sides became deadlocked. When authorities in the north ignored a United Nations resolution for supervised elections in 1948, a pro-Western government was established in the south (the Republic of Korea). Later the Soviet Union established the Democratic People's Republic of Korea in the north. In June 1949, U.S. troops withdrew.

One year later, North Korean forces invaded South Korea. A United Nations–backed coalition of sixteen member nations sent assistance to South Korea. The resulting war lasted three years and ended in a stalemate. On July 27, 1953, an armistice agreement was signed and a Military Armistice Commission with five members for each side was set up to supervise the implementation of the armistice. Neither the USA nor South Korea ever signed the agreement (although they respect the terms as members of the United Nations), so a state of war is formally still in effect.

The United States of America still maintains a military presence in South Korea, although feelings that this should end are growing.

The year 1980 marked the beginning of Korea's focused development of a high-tech industry. It was also the year of the Kwangju massacre, when government troops killed hundreds of demonstrators who were part of a prodemocracy movement. In 1988 Seoul hosted the Olympic games (when restaurants removed dog from their menus in deference to delicate Western sensibilities), and Korea held their first free parliamentary elections. South (and North) Korea joined the United Nations in 1991, and in 2000, former president Kim Dae Jung received the Nobel Peace Prize. In 2004, a site was chosen for the new capital city in the Yeongi-Kwangju area.

Cultural Note

Prior to the 1950s, North Korea was the industrial heartland of the peninsula. However, their industries have been dwarfed by South Korea's modernization. Nighttime satellite photos prove how different the economies of North and South Korea have become. At night, Seoul is a brilliantly lit site in the glowing, prosperous southern half of the peninsula. In contrast, North Korea's lights are sporadic and dim—mute evidence of the slower development of North Korea.

Type of Government

South Korea is a unitary multiparty republic, governed by a president, prime minister, deputy prime minister, and State Council (cabinet). There is also a unicameral National Assembly and a Supreme Court.

The prime minister is the head of the government. The chief of state is the president, who is elected to a five-year term. Members of the National Assembly serve a four-year term.

Current government data can be found at the Embassy of South Korea at *www.koreaembassyusa.org*.

Language

Korean is the official language of South Korea. English is widely taught in schools. Therefore, businesspeople are often familiar with English, especially in urban areas.

Korean is a Ural-Altaic language, but, unlike Japanese and Chinese, Korean does not use tones. Approximately 1,300 Chinese characters are used in modern Korean. The literacy rate is 92 percent, and newspaper readership is very high in South Korea.

Cultural Note

Which of the following is the correct method of transliterating the twenty-four-letter Korean alphabet into the twenty-six-letter Roman alphabet?

- The McCune-Reischauer method
- The Korean government's method
- Everyone else's method
- All of the above

The correct answer is "all of the above." Because of the variety of transliterations, Korean words can be spelled multiple ways in English.

The South Korean View

Dominant religions include Confucianism, Christianity (26 percent of the population), Buddhism, Shamanism (spirit worship), and Chondokyo (religion of the heavenly way). South Korea is a society run along Confucian precepts. In fact, Confucianism may have had a more profound effect on Korea than it had even in China, where Confucianism originated. (Remember that Confucianism is not a religion in the classic sense of the word. Rather, it is a philosophy and guide for living.)

Confucius taught that the basic unit of society is the family. In order to preserve harmony in the home, certain reciprocal responsibilities must be preserved in relationships. These relationships are between ruler and subjects, between husband and wife, between father and son, between elder brother and younger brother, and between friends. Because all but the last are hierarchical, rank and age are very important in all interactions. While all actions of the individual reflect upon the family, filial piety is of utmost importance. Virtues of kindness, righteousness, propriety, intelligence, and faithfulness are also revered.

The only relationships of equality in Korea are between members of the same class. One's closest friends are drawn from this group.

Korea has no official religion. Buddhism has traditionally been the major Korean religion, but Buddhism has gone through periods where it has been repressed by Korea's Confucian rulers. Buddhism is Korea's most popular religion, although only about 26 percent of Koreans identify themselves as Buddhist. (About half of Koreans follow no formal religion at all.)

Koreans are proud that Christianity did not reach Korea through missionaries. Instead, a Korean scholar studying in Beijing was baptized a Catholic in 1777. It was this scholar, on his return, who introduced Catholicism to Korea. Protestantism gained a foothold in 1884, via a Protestant physician who became the royal physician.

Whatever their formal religion, most Koreans also follow traditional Shamanistic beliefs. These include a belief in spirits, the veneration of ancestors, and the usefulness of fortunetelling. If there is one classic Korean characteristic, it would be resiliency. Koreans seem to be able to survive almost any hardship. Sacrifice has been demanded of one generation after another of Koreans. The results of this sacrifice in South Korea are evident to any visitor: a poor, war-torn agricultural country with few resources has transformed itself into the twelfth largest economy in the world.

☑ Know Before You Go

Korea suffers from occasional typhoons and low-level seismic activity. Air pollution is an issue in large cities, along with minor crimes like burglaries and pickpocketing.

Overall, Korea's crime rate is low; however, only use legitimate taxis or public transportation.

Avoid demonstrations; they can become confrontational and violent.

Cultural Note

South Korea is one of the most crowded nations on Earth—it is even more densely populated than India or Japan. In such a crowded country, personal space is limited. Koreans are accustomed to standing or sitting close together. On the street, they compete aggressively, bumping each other and treading on feet without apology. Since such contact is unintentional, Koreans do not feel the need to apologize for such behavior.

▶ CULTURAL ORIENTATION

Cognitive Styles: How South Koreans Organize and Process Information

In South Korea, one finds a culture that is closed to many foreign influences. Its basic education teaches one to think associatively and subjectively. In all situations, personal involvement is stronger than the rules and laws one might use to control behavior.

Negotiation Strategies: What South Koreans Accept as Evidence

One's personal feelings about an issue have traditionally been perceived as the truth. The use of objective facts is becoming more common in negotiations. Faith in the ideologies of nationalism may have some influence on an individual's view.

Value Systems: The Basis for Behavior

Koreans are strong adherents of Confucianism. They strive to build a society in which individuals are aware of their relative position, fulfill their obligations to superiors with obedience and respect, and recognize their responsibility to treat inferiors with justice and benevolence. The following three sections identify the Value Systems in the predominant culture—their methods of dividing right from wrong, good from evil, and so forth.

Locus of Decision-Making

This is a collectivistic culture in which the individual may speak for the group, but decisions are made by a consensus of the group, with deference given to the one in the group who has the highest ethos—usually the oldest member. Loyalty to kin always supersedes loyalty to friends, neighbors, or the state. The self is downplayed, but Western-style individualism is felt. One must not cause another person to be embarrassed, so an outright "no" is rarely used.

Sources of Anxiety Reduction

The nuclear family is the basic unit of society, but the extended family gives stability and security to its members. There is a very strong work ethic, but intragroup harmony must also be maintained. Giving gifts to acquire favors is a common practice in the workplace, and reciprocity is expected. Friends expect to rely on each other for everything. They spend a lot of time together, and friendships last a lifetime.

Issues of Equality/Inequality

In business, the emphasis is on entry-level skills and team play. There is an inherent trust in people because of the homogeneity of the populace and social pressure. This produces a strong feeling of interdependency among members of a group or business. Age is revered. Respect and deference are directed from the younger to the older, and authority and responsibility from the older to the younger. There are clearly differentiated sex roles in society, but Western-style equality is creeping in and there is a strong feminist movement. Men still generally dominate in public situations.

Cultural Note

Faux Pas: A foreign manufacturer of dog food experienced delay after delay in his efforts to put dog food commercials on South Korean television. Only after months of fruitless effort did the company discover the reason for the opposition: Too many South Koreans still remember hunger and poverty. When people do not have enough food, South Koreans consider it shameful to promote a special food for dogs. Although there has been no famine in South Korea in decades, the memory of it is still present—and famine is still endemic in North Korea.

⊙ BUSINESS PRACTICES

Punctuality, Appointments, and Local Time

- Business hours are generally 9:00 A.M. to 5:00 P.M., Monday through Friday, and often 9:00 A.M. to 1:00 P.M. on Saturday.
- Be punctual to meetings. This is expected from foreigners as a sign of good business practice. Do not get upset, however, if your counterpart is late.
- Punctuality is also expected at social events.

- Koreans often arrange one-on-one business meetings (as opposed to the Japanese, who prefer group meetings). Nevertheless, this one Korean businessperson will have to sell your proposal to his or her entire company. It is important that you establish a strong relationship with your contact person.
- Age and rank are very important in Korea. It is sometimes easier to establish a rapport with a businessperson your own age.
- When entering a group meeting, the senior member of your party should enter the conference room first, then the next-highest-ranking person, and so on. The Koreans will be lined up inside in order of importance.
- English is the most widely studied foreign language. Your business meetings can be conducted in English. Promotional materials and correspondence may be in English as well.
- The best times for business meetings are usually 10:00 to 11:00 A.M. and 2:00 to 3:00 P.M. Prior appointments are necessary. Business dinners are common.
- Korean businesspeople vacation from mid-July to mid-August; avoid trying to schedule appointments at this time of year. Other bad times include early October, a time of many holidays, and Christmastime.
- Many Asians write the day first, then the month, then the year (e.g., December 3, 2010, is written 3.12.10 or 3/12/10).
- For a list of the official holidays of South Korea, visit *www.kissbow orshakehands.com.*
- Local time is nine hours ahead of Greenwich Mean Time (G.M.T. + 9), or fourteen hours ahead of U.S. Eastern Standard Time (E.S.T. + 14).

Cultural Note

The basis for a successful business relationship in South Korea is a respectful rapport between individuals. Personal relationships take precedence over business. Businesses are basically conservative and have a strong work ethic. Harmony and structure are emphasized over innovation and experimentation. Be sincere and honest in business dealings. Meet face-to-face and keep in touch after your trip by e-mail and telephone.

Negotiating

- At each meeting, take time to talk to your counterpart. The first meeting should be solely for that purpose; never jump right into business discussions. Expect tea to be served at the beginning of the meeting; it is good manners to accept this sign of hospitality. Retain your formality as long as your counterpart does; do not become "chummy."

- Do not be fooled into thinking that Korea is completely westernized because of its façade of modernization. While the younger generation is open to globalization, traditional values run deep, especially with the older generation. You may find younger executives easier to negotiate with, as they will follow more westernized patterns.

- Business will tend to take place at a slower pace than in Europe or North America. Be patient with delays in decision-making. Often, this is a tactic to wear down the other side. Therefore, do not talk about your deadlines. Expect to make several trips to Korea before reaching an agreement.

- Do not be surprised if a Korean executive does not call you back immediately when you notify his or her office of a problem. Korean employees are very protective of their supervisors' harmony, and traditionally will not upset their boss with a problem until the timing is just right. This is especially true at the start of the workday.

- Find out who will be included in the negotiating team for the other side and match the rank of the persons represented. Status is very important, and a mismatch may prove embarrassing to both sides. Generally, representatives should be older and hold senior positions in the company.

- Although this is changing, it is still not common to have women participate in business in Korea. This means that women will have the additional challenge of overcoming an initial hesitancy. It is best to consider this factor and mention to your Korean contact that a woman will be included in the team. This will allow them some time to adjust to the situation.

- Negotiations in Korea will be much more emotional than in Western countries that stress logic and the bottom-line cost. Mutual trust and compatibility will be the basis of a good business relationship. Also be prepared for the style to be aggressive at times. Koreans are much more direct and quicker to express anger or frustration. Remain calm yourself, and do not take everything said during these sessions seriously.

- Consider sending your proposals in advance of your visit for your host to preview. At a presentation, recap the major points at the beginning and the end. Break up the information into small segments with pauses and question-and-answer periods in between. Be patient with extensive questioning. Address the chief negotiator occasionally, even if he does not speak English. Do not use triangular shapes in your promotional material, because triangles have negative connotations.

- Look for cues that your counterpart did not understand you. Silence is one such sign.

- Do not ask or expect Koreans to tell you when this happens, as it will embarrass them. Instead, rephrase your statement or inquire if they would like more information.

- The use of a translator is recommended to avoid these kinds of miscommunications.

- Make a beginning bid that will leave you plenty of room to negotiate. Your counterparts will start off with an extreme position but will be prepared to meet you in the middle. This way both sides come away having gained a lot of ground.

- Brute honesty is not appreciated in Korea. While a direct "no" is more accepted in Korea than in other Asian countries, Koreans are not as direct as many Westerners. In order to avoid saying "no," Koreans will often give the answer they think the other wants to hear. It is more important to leave you with good feelings than to be accurate and cause you dismay. Therefore, learn to listen to subtleties by asking questions that do not require a yes or no answer. A "yes" or nod of the head may mean "maybe" or "I understand." A "maybe" usually means "no." A negative response is sometimes indicated by a squint of the eyes or by tipping the head back while drawing air in through the teeth and waiting for you to speak again.

- Be sensitive to the overall length of the meeting. If the Koreans appear curious, take this lead and pursue it. If they return to social chitchat, take this as a sign that they are finished discussing business for the day.
- Bow at the beginning and end of a meeting. An exit bow that is longer than the greeting bow is an indication that the meeting went well.
- Avoid being loud and boisterous around Koreans. Although they are more direct than most Asians, they dislike rowdy behavior.
- Treat the elderly with respect. Acknowledge them first in a group, and do not smoke or wear sunglasses when they are near. If you meet in a doorway, allow the older person to pass through first.
- Modesty is very important. Do not enter a home or office until you are invited, and do not seat yourself until you are asked to do so. Wait for the invitation to be extended several times before accepting. Be modest about your position and accomplishments in your company, and if you receive a compliment, politely refute it. Expect others to do the same. This should not stop you from complimenting another, however, as compliments are appreciated.
- Not losing "face"—the dignity of another person—is a very important and delicate matter. Therefore, never embarrass another person, especially in public. Never criticize your competition or admit that you do not know the answer to a question.
- Do not confuse Korean history and culture with those of any of its Asian neighbors. Korea has a distinctive language, history, and culture, and they are very proud of this. This pride and sense of history is quite strong and constitutes a large part of their self-image. Koreans are especially sensitive about Japan, so do not bring gifts from Japan or make reference to personal contacts there.
- If the Korean national anthem is played in a public place, stand at attention out of respect.
- Be careful not to overly admire an object belonging to another person; he or she may feel obliged to give it to you.
- Contacts are important in Korea. Koreans tend to be suspicious of people they do not know, or people with whom they do not have a mutual contact. Try to obtain a personal introduction.

- Be prepared to give out a lot of business cards. Have your name, company, and title printed in English on one side and in Korean on the reverse. Cards are very important, since they indicate your rank and are a key to the respect you deserve in their culture.
- Offer your card with your right hand. Never place a Korean's card in your wallet if you intend to put your wallet in your back pocket. Never write on a business card.
- Do not sign a contract or write a person's name in red ink. To many Buddhists, this indicates that the person is deceased.
- Do not be surprised if you are asked personal questions, such as how much you paid for something or your salary. These questions are not considered in bad taste in Korea and often reflect an attempt to determine your rank and status.
- Attempts by foreigners to adhere to Korean modes of etiquette will not go unnoticed and may be instrumental in your eventual business success.

Cultural Note

Faux Pas: In 1998, the Swedish automobile firm Volvo bought 85 percent of Samsung's construction equipment business. Volvo's corporate culture is very different from that of the average Korean firm. In particular, Volvo tried to institute its culture of transparency, sharing all its plans with its employees in the hope that they will offer useful suggestions. It was expected that Volvo's Korean employees would keep the corporation's plans secret. They did not. Male Korean executives, like Japanese executives, spend most nights drinking and singing karaoke with their friends. In Korea, these friends will be a group of people who graduated from the same college in the same year. Some of them may work for competing companies. Information that should be proprietorial tends to leak during these drinking sessions. Volvo is not the only foreign firm to have had problems in this arena.

Business Entertaining

- The largest meal of the day is eaten in the evening, usually between 6:00 and 8:00 P.M.
- Entertaining is most often done in a restaurant or coffee shop; rarely is it done at home. If you are invited to a home, consider this an honor. Do not discuss business during a meal unless your

host brings it up first. Do not expect to be shown around the house, and do not wander about the home or look in such rooms as the kitchen.

- Remove your shoes when entering a Korean home, restaurant, or temple building. Leave them with the toes pointing away from the building. When putting your shoes back on, do not sit with your back toward the temple.

- Call ahead before visiting a home. When taking your leave, express your thanks and bow slightly. Send a thank-you note to your host after a meal. It is polite to reciprocate by inviting your host to a meal of equal value at a later date.

- It is common to be invited out after business hours to a bar or dinner where there will be a lot of alcohol. This is an important part of establishing an informal relationship and judging character. The alcohol is a stimulus to expression of more direct opinions; however, all comments and promises made during these times will be taken seriously afterward. Do not refuse these invitations, and do not bring your spouse. Try to reciprocate before you leave.

- The person who invites the other(s) is expected to pay for the meal. It is polite for the younger to pay for the older. In all cases, a good-natured argument over who will pay is expected.

- Koreans eat a lot of garlic in their food. The smell is emitted from the skin. In getting used to this, remember that Koreans may find the odors emitted from red meat eaters, or heavy caffeine drinkers, offensive. Remember that the sense of olfaction is in a primitive part of the brain, and any strong reaction you may have to different scents should be guarded. Asian cultures that do not eat a large amount of dairy products may find the odor, consistency, and digestion of cheese difficult to handle.

- When sitting on the floor for a meal, men should cross their legs while sitting on the cushion. Women (and men) may sit with their legs to the side, but never straightened out under the table.

- Koreans use chopsticks for eating and a porcelain spoon for soup. Your attempts at using chopsticks will be appreciated. When you are finished, set your chopsticks on the chopstick rest. Placing them parallel on top of your bowl is considered a sign of bad luck, and leaving them sticking out of rice is in bad taste, because this is how offerings are made to ancestors.

- Pass food with your right hand, supported by your left. Do not be shocked to see unusual foods. (There are many delicacies in Korea which might surprise a Western palate). It is polite to refill your neighbor's cup and soy sauce bowl when empty; expect the same. Drinking partners will often trade filled cups to drink. If you do not want a refill, do not finish your glass.

- Do not put food taken from a serving dish directly into your mouth. Transfer it to your plate or bowl first. Never pick up food with your fingers. Even fruit is eaten in slices with chopsticks.

- At a meal, do not finish everything on your plate. This indicates that you are still hungry and that the host did not provide enough for you. The host will offer more food several times. Even if you want more, refuse at least twice before accepting more. If you are hosting a party, offer food at least three times.

- At the end of a meal, there may be singing. It is impolite to refuse to sing if asked.

- Good topics of conversation include Korea's cultural heritage (which is extensive), kites, sports (especially the Olympics), and the health of the other's family (although family inquiries on topics other than health are considered an intrusion). Topics to avoid are local politics (discussions of which may be forbidden by the government for reasons of national security), socialism, Communism, Japan, and your host's wife.

Cultural Note

"Without question, the trait that sets Koreans apart from the Chinese, Japanese, and other Asians is their emotionalism. . . . They are quick to anger and just as quick to reconciliation. They are the only Asians among whom you will commonly see public tears or public displays of affection. . . ."

"Korean men are very emotional even when making business decisions. If you strike the right emotional cord, the Korean decision-maker will often respond favorably simply on impulse. On the other hand, a Korean, unlike Japanese, will not be polite when you get on his wrong side. Korean tempers can get awfully hot. . . ."

—From *The Asian Mind Game* by Chin-ning Chu

▶ PROTOCOL

Greetings

- Korean men greet each other with a slight bow and sometimes an accompanying handshake while maintaining eye contact. Indicate added respect by supporting your right forearm with your left hand during the handshake.
- The junior person will initiate the greetings and be the first to bow. The senior person will be the first to offer his hand. A gentle handshake or nod of the head may be sufficient in business circles. Women rarely shake hands. Generally, men should not try to shake hands with Korean women; Western women will have to initiate a handshake with Korean men.
- Elderly people are very highly respected, so it is polite to greet them first—and spend a few minutes speaking with them.
- A compliment on an elder's good health is always appreciated.
- Wait to be introduced to another at gatherings and parties. Avoid introducing yourself, and employ a third person if there is someone you wish to meet.

Titles/Forms of Address

- Traditionally, a Korean person had a family name, a generational or clan name, and a given—or first—name (in that order). For example, Kim Hyong-Sim has the family name of Kim, the generational name of Hyong, and a first name of Sim. While this is confusing to Westerners, our system is equally confusing to them, so they too may mix Western names around.
- Korean family names tend to be one-syllable, while generational names are more likely to be two-syllable.
- Note that family names can be transliterated into English in several ways; in English, the surname Lee might be Rhee, Yi, Li, or Lee.
- Address people by their title alone or by both their title and their family name. Kim Hyong-Sim would be referred to as Mr. Kim, Kim Sonsaengnim (meaning "Mr." or "teacher") or Kimssi, with the suffix -*ssi* added, which can mean "Mr.," "Mrs.," or "Miss." Given names are not used unless permission is granted to do so.

- Married women will keep their maiden names. If you do not know a woman's maiden name, it is permissible to refer to her as "Madame" with her husband's family name.
- Never write a Korean's name in red ink. Korean Buddhists only write a dead person's name in red ink (either at the time of their death or at the anniversary of a death).

Gestures
- Do not put your arm around another person's shoulders. People of the same sex may hold hands. Physical contact is inappropriate with older people, with people of the opposite sex, or with people who are not good friends or family.
- Feet are considered dirty and should not touch other people or objects. Men should keep their feet flat on the floor during formal situations. At other times men should take care that the soles of their shoes are pointing down. Women are permitted to cross their legs.
- Show respect to older people by touching your left hand, palm up, lightly to your right elbow when shaking hands or passing objects such as food or documents.
- Get someone's attention by extending your arm palm down and moving your fingers up and down. Beckoning a person by moving a single finger toward you is very rude.
- Cover your mouth when yawning or using a toothpick. It is not necessary to cover your mouth when laughing, as many Korean women do.
- Blowing your nose in public is considered gauche. If the highly spiced Korean food affects you, get up and move away from the table before blowing your nose.
- If embarrassed, a Korean may laugh excessively.
- Intermittent eye contact is important to convey sincerity and attentiveness to the speaker.

Gifts
- When visiting a family, it is appropriate to bring a gift of fruit, imported coffee, or quality tea such as ginseng, chocolates, or crafts from home. Liquor may be given to a man but never to a woman.

- Gift giving is often practiced within a business setting. Good gifts for a first trip include impersonal products with your company logo on them. (Be sure these gifts were not produced in Korea or Japan.)
- When giving or receiving a gift, use both hands. The gift is not opened in the presence of the giver. A gift of money should be put in an envelope. Expect initial resistance to receiving a gift. This is polite, so be persistent.

Cultural Note

It is customary to reciprocate a gift with one of similar value. Therefore, choose a gift that takes into account the receiver's economic means. If you receive such an extravagant gift that you cannot reciprocate, consider sending it back, being very careful not to offend the sender. Indicate that the sender's generosity is great and the gift is too much.

Dress

- Men should wear a conservative suit and tie and a white shirt for business.
- Fashions are changing for women; they may wear a conservative suit, pantsuit, skirt and blouse, or dress. Whatever you select, avoid tight skirts, because many people sit on the floor in homes and restaurants.
- Dress modestly for informal times. Revealing clothing for women will be a mark of poor character. Shorts are appropriate for young people. Avoid the colors yellow and pink.

Cultural Note

Nepotism is common in Korea: securing jobs for relatives was traditionally a goal of the successful executive. This, like many traditions, may be changing. In April of 1999, Kim Dae Jung of South Korea denounced nepotism in the management of Korean Air—an airline with one of the world's worst safety records. "Korean Air is a typical case of management gone wrong with family members in its top managerial posts," noted President Kim. Although Korean Air is a private airline, President Kim believes that the airline's poor record reflects badly upon the Republic of Korea. At the time of this speech, Korean Air was the world's thirteenth largest airline.

Sri Lanka

Democratic Socialist Republic of Sri Lanka
Former: Serendib, Ceylon

Cultural Note

The 2004 tsunami devastated this exquisite island. Tens of thousands of people perished, property was decimated, and the economy was crippled. Relief programs will go on for years, but the tragedy will have an effect for generations.

▶ WHAT'S YOUR CULTURAL IQ?

1. A famous Buddhist temple in Sri Lanka contains a very holy object. What is it?
    a. Buddha's robes
    b. Buddha's dagger
    c. Buddha's tooth
    ANSWER: c. The Buddha (who lived sometime around 563 to 483 B.C.) was said to have visited Sri Lanka three times, and his tooth is a prized relic in the Temple of the Tooth, the holiest Buddhist shrine in the country. This temple was damaged in 1998 by an LTTE (Liberation Tigers of Tamil Eelam) truck bomb.

2. TRUE or FALSE: The rupee is the official currency in Sri Lanka.
    ANSWER: TRUE. It is divided into 100 cents.

3. Match the Sri Lankan dishes with their main ingredients.
    a. Sambols   1. Meat, fish, or vegetables
    b. Mallung   2. Hot chilies, fish, and lime juice
    c. Curry   3. Shredded leaves, coconut, onions, lime juice
    ANSWER: a. 2 (Sambols can scorch your tongue); b. 3 (Mallung is milder, and the flavors depend upon the leaves); c. 1 (a curry's contents can range from lentils to lamb).

▶ TIPS ON DOING BUSINESS IN SRI LANKA

- The largest ethnic population in Sri Lanka are the Sinhalese, who are usually Buddhists. Tamils, who make up about 20 percent of the population, are generally Hindus (or Muslims). Consider their belief systems when you conduct business, or entertain them. For instance, Buddhists are generally vegetarians, Hindus do not eat beef, and Muslims do not eat pork.

- Meals are important events, and should be shared with your Sri Lankan counterparts as often as possible.

- Try local cuisines, and definitely learn about their tea. Tea plantations are placed at high altitudes for the cool air, and the handpicked teas grown at the highest elevation are regarded as premium.

- Time is flexible in Sri Lanka. Westerners will be expected to consider time money, but your Sri Lankan counterparts will not share your attitude.

- The tsunami has touched innumerable lives in Sri Lanka, from the way they view daily life, to work, to how they eat. For example, even though many Sri Lankans would normally eat fish, the catches remained untouched in many markets during 2005, because the shoppers were afraid that the fish have been feeding on the carcasses of the thousands of relatives who were swept away to sea.

- Highly aggressive negotiating tactics are not commonplace. The relationship and trust that your business partner has with you is more important than the concrete margins of your deal. All parties should benefit from every agreement in the business matters that you are involved in.

Cultural Note

During the British colonial occupation (in the 1800s), coffee was Sri Lanka's main crop. However, most of the coffee crop was decimated by a leaf blight in the 1870s, so the mainstay coffee plantations were replaced by tea and rubber. Sri Lanka and India are now the two largest exporters of tea in the world.

▶ COUNTRY BACKGROUND

Demographics

Of Sri Lanka's 20 million inhabitants (2006 estimate), 74 percent are Sinhalese, 18 percent are Tamil, 7 percent are Moor, and 1 percent are Burgher (descendants of Dutch colonists), Malay, and Vedda. The Veddas are a small remnant of the island's original inhabitants who have assimilated into Sri Lankan society and lost all traces of their original culture and history. Ethnic divisions between the Sinhalese and the Tamils run deep, and violent strife has been a problem since 1983. Tamils are generally concentrated in the "tea country," the northern part of the island.

History

The first Sinhalese immigrants to Sri Lanka arrived in the sixth century from northern India. Three hundred years later, Buddhism was brought with the Indian prince Mahinda, son of the great Buddhist king Asoka. The religion flourished and became central to the culture.

The Portuguese were the first Europeans to arrive in Sri Lanka in the sixteenth century; they brought Catholicism with them. The Dutch followed in the next century, and finally the British arrived and declared it the British colony of Ceylon in 1815. During this colonial period, tea, rubber, and coconut plantations were established in the northern part of the island, and labor was brought over from the Tamil Nadu province in India. Sri Lanka's independence was peacefully obtained on February 4, 1948.

Since that time, free elections have been the vehicle for transfer of power, with the exception of the assassination of Prime Minister Bandaranaike in 1959. In 1971, an uprising of a Maoist group caused the government, under Bandaranaike's widow, to declare a state of emergency and suppress the insurrection. Although the revolt was put down in a few weeks, the state of emergency lasted six years. Partially in response to the turbulence, a new constitution was written that changed the country to a republic and its name to Sri Lanka. In addition, it created a presidency (appointed by the prime minister) and initiated economic policies that were highly socialistic.

In 1977, a change in political parties brought a new constitution and an open economy under J. R. Jayewardene. At that point, the Tamils' demand for more equalization at the federal level changed to a demand for an independent state of Tamil Eelam. The extremist LTTE resorted to force to achieve their goals. In 1983, the deaths of thirteen Sinhalese soldiers caused violent confrontations. Bloodshed, terrorism, and accusations of human rights violations occurred on both sides.

In 1987, the situation was deadlocked. India became involved by sending peacekeeping troops to help resolve the crisis. An accord was signed that made concessions to some of the militants' demands, including giving official status to the Tamil language. But the militant troops backed out on their agreement to surrender to the Indian peacekeeping force. The fighting continued, and Indian troops remained in northern Sri Lanka for two years.

After the negotiated Indian withdrawal occurred in 1990, elections were held in the newly restructured provinces. With the resulting victory in Tamil strongholds and the seats won in the National Assembly, the militants halted activities. However, fighting broke out again in June 1990. Several hundred people were killed before a cease-fire was declared.

Since then, the LTTE terrorist activities have continued their political violence, including assassinations of politicians, bombings, and attacks on religious sites. In spite of these hostilities, the country is relatively stable politically.

The government has sold over fifty state-owned companies in recent years, and Colombo has a modern stock exchange. If international aid continues, and the plans for growth in the telecom and financial services areas can be implemented, Sri Lanka will regain its economic position in the next few years.

Type of Government
The Democratic Socialist Republic of Sri Lanka is a unitary multiparty republic. Under the constitution of 1978, there is a strong executive president, elected for a six-year term, and a prime minister. There is a unicameral National Assembly. The president is head of both the state and the government.

Internationally, Sri Lanka maintains a nonaligned foreign policy. Relations with India, which have been tense in the past, remain a focus of attention.

Current government data can be found at the Embassy of Sri Lanka at *www.slembassyusa.org* or the official Web site of the government of Sri Lanka at *www.priu.gov.lk*.

Language

Sri Lanka has two official languages, spoken by the two dominant ethnic groups. The Sinhalese speak Sinhala, and the Tamils speak Tamil. English, a legacy from the colonial period, is the language of commerce and is spoken in tourist areas, and most businesspeople and senior civil servants speak it fluently. For data on the various languages of Sri Lanka, see Ethnologue at *www.ethnologue.com*.

Cultural Note

Although its influence is declining, a caste system (called *jati*, or "birth," in Asia) still exists in Sri Lanka. This system dictates a person's social standing, occupation, and even marriage possibilities. While there are only four traditional castes, these are broken down into thousands of subcastes. The concept of purity is integral to the caste system. Not just physical purity, but spiritual—which leads to personal enlightenment as the ultimate goal. The preservation of psychic purity was historically a main reason for segregating interaction between castes.

The Sri Lankan View

When Buddhism went into decline in India, Sri Lanka emerged as a Buddhist stronghold in southern Asia. The majority of the population claim Buddhism as their religion. Of the remaining citizenry, approximately 20 percent are Hindu, with the remaining being Christians and Muslims.

Buddhism is a strongly held belief system, which can be interpreted in various ways. Briefly, Buddhists follow the teachings of Buddha; they believe in the dharma (the truth, the law or the teaching); and they belong to the sangha (the community). Buddhism has many precepts that are explained beautifully in hundreds of books, and dozens of Web sites.

If visitors to Sri Lanka would like to learn more about Buddhism, there are various centers and societies around Kandy which offer options for study and meditation. Visit the government's Web site listed previously for further information.

Precepts of Hinduism are discussed in the chapter on India.

☑ Know Before You Go

A number of high visibility, politically motivated abductions and murders took place during the cease-fire agreement in 2005. One incident involved D. Sivaram, a columnist at the *Daily Mirror,* and editor of TamilNet. There are ongoing investigations into his and other murders.

Buses are a common mode of transportation; however, they can be hazardous. In April of 2005, a bus that tried to beat a train resulted in the death of thirty-seven passengers. The bus driver survived to face murder charges.

Certain areas are still heavily mined, and others are sometimes unsafe for business travelers to visit because of the political difficulties between the government and the "Tamil Tigers." Check for travel advisories before you venture into dense rural regions.

▶ CULTURAL ORIENTATION

Cognitive Styles: How Sri Lanka's Citizens Organize and Process Information

In Sri Lanka, both the Sinhalese and the Tamils are open to new methods and innovations, except when those methods or innovations come from the opposite ethnic group. Most education is skill training, and there is little abstraction. Generally, Sri Lankans tend to behave in ways that are dictated by tradition and the situation of the moment. Interpersonal relationships are more important than abstract rules in the conduct of business.

Negotiation Strategies: What the citizens of Sri Lanka Accept as Evidence

Both the Sinhalese (Buddhists) and the Tamils (Hindus) will use faith in the ideologies of their religion as a foundation for truth, modified by their personal feelings about an issue. Objective facts are seldom regarded as the sole possible source of evidence.

Value Systems: The Basis for Behavior

In Sri Lanka, there are two ethnic groups, the Sinhalese and the Tamils, whose values and goals clash constantly. The following three sections identify the Value Systems in these predominant cultures—their methods of dividing right from wrong, good from evil, and so forth.

Locus of Decision-Making

The concern of the Sinhalese is with one's responsibility to self and to interpersonal relationships, while the Tamils' concern is with one's responsibility to the collective—family, group, religion. Identity for both is found in the social system. Thus, individual decisions are made with social position in mind. There is a need for prestige within the group, so ranking is important.

Sources of Anxiety Reduction

The family is the central social unit in both groups and gives the individual the most security. Religious and ethnic affiliations (nearly synonymous terms) give the individual and his or her family the structure for their life. A strong patrilineal kinship system assures continuity and family stability. A high level of religious tolerance helps to offset the anxiety of ethnic differences.

Issues of Equality/Inequality

There is a strong feeling of inequality between the majority Sinhalese and the minority Tamils, leading to active insurrection and terrorism. The caste system exists but is not rigidly adhered to. Although ethnic groups desire segregation, government policy is to treat all people as equals. Men dominate most aspects of business and public life and are the heads of their family units. There are clear and classic role differences between the sexes.

▶ BUSINESS PRACTICES

Punctuality, Appointments, and Local Time

- Business hours are 8:30 A.M. to 4:30 or 5:00 P.M., Monday through Friday. Some companies close for lunch between noon and 2:00 P.M.

- Punctuality is considered important and expected from Westerners. Do not be surprised, however, if your counterpart is late or keeps you waiting.
- Urban areas in Sri Lanka have heavy traffic during rush hours. Allow plenty of time between appointments for travel.
- Sri Lankans have a much more relaxed attitude about time than do North Americans.
- Most Sri Lankans would not object to a two- or three-hour wait before seeing an important person. Do not display anger if you are made to wait.
- As a foreigner, you must make appointments at least one week in advance. Also, reconfirm your appointments a day or two before. (Native Sri Lankans, however, often drop in on one another without appointments.)
- Sri Lankans take a "tea break" both in the morning and in the afternoon. Don't expect help from any employees during their tea break, even if they are sitting at their desks. No business is conducted during the tea break.
- Many introductory business appointments are held over meals. Lunch in a restaurant is a common first appointment, but lunch or dinner in a Sri Lankan home is not unusual.
- Most Sri Lankan holidays are connected with the country's four main religions: Buddhism, Hinduism, Islam, and Christianity. For a list of the official holidays of Sri Lanka, visit *www.kissbowor shakehands.com.*
- Local time is 5 ½ hours ahead of Greenwich Mean Time (G.M.T. + 5 ½), or 10 ½ hours ahead of U.S. Eastern Standard Time (E.S.T. + 10 ½).

Negotiating
- It is important to establish a rapport with your counterpart before jumping into business discussions. Therefore, take time to talk socially before starting negotiations. Be patient with delays, and do not expect business to move as quickly as in Western countries. Several trips to Sri Lanka may be necessary to finalize a deal.

- If you are served tea at the beginning of a meeting, always accept this as a goodwill gesture and make a compliment on its quality.
- Do not be surprised if your Sinhalese counterparts consult with an astrologer before making any important commitments.
- Women are moving into more senior business positions; however, there are not as many female executives as in the West.
- Business cards are often exchanged at first meetings. Have your cards printed in English. Having the local language printed on the reverse side is a good idea only if you can distinguish between a Tamil and a Sinhalese. Since this can be difficult for foreigners, it may be better to leave it off.
- The caste system is still a way of life in many areas. It is important to respect this aspect of the culture and realize that there are places and activities where some people are not accepted. Do not pressure a person to violate this set of beliefs.
- As in most countries, Sri Lankans write the day first, then the month, and then the year (e.g., December 3, 2010, is written 3.12.10 or 3/12/10).

Cultural Note

Treat religious objects with the utmost respect. Do not sit or stand on large statues of Buddha or otherwise handle images of Buddha sacrilegiously. Do not give Buddhist monks money directly, since they are forbidden to touch it; instead, place donations in the box found at the entrance to the temple. Hand any other object to a monk with both hands.

When visiting a mosque or temple, wear clothing that covers your legs and arms (both men and women), and remove your shoes and hat at the door. Remember, leather articles may be restricted.

Business Entertaining

- It will not be uncommon for you to be invited to a local home for a visit or a meal. If this happens, it is polite to reciprocate with a meal in a restaurant in your hotel.
- It is not impolite to drop by unannounced. The best times to visit are between 4:00 and 7:00 P.M.

- Meal times are usually 7:00 to 8:00 A.M. for breakfast, noon to 2:00 P.M. for lunch, and 7:00 to 10:00 P.M. for dinner.
- Be prepared for as much as two or three hours of talking and socializing before a meal. It is advisable to have a small snack before going.
- At a meal, communal dishes are placed in the center of the table and each person serves himself or herself. Do not let the serving utensils touch your plate, and never use your left hand. Usually, there will be no utensils, as people eat with their hands. Bread and rice balls are used to scoop up curries and vegetables. Watch your host. This technique takes a bit of practice. If your meal is served on a plantain leaf, do not eat it; that plantain leaf is your plate.
- Do not serve yourself large portions, but leave room to compliment your host and hostess by returning for two or three helpings. When you are finished, politely refuse additional servings.
- Buddhists are vegetarians, Hindus do not eat beef, and Muslims do not eat pork. When eating out, the person who initiates the invitation is the one who will pay for the entire meal.
- Good topics of conversation include families, home, schools, and sights of Sri Lanka. Topics to avoid include the ethnic strife between the Tamils and Sinhalese, relations with India, religion, the caste system, sex, and the tragedies of the tsunami.
- If the topic of the tsunami is broached by your Sri Lankan associates, be very sensitive to their viewpoints about the disaster, but refrain from offering your opinions on rebuilding, international aid, etc.

▶ PROTOCOL

Greetings
- The traditional greeting is to place your hands together at chin level and bow slightly.
- Foreigners are not expected to initiate this gesture, but returning it will be appreciated.
- As a result of British influence, the Western mode of greeting, shaking hands, is also appropriate for either sex.
- At a party, greet and shake hands with everyone in the room.

Titles/Forms of Address

- Each of Sri Lanka's many cultures has different naming patterns. Depending upon whether they are Sinhalese, Tamil, Moor (Arabic or Malay), Burgher, etc., they will have a variety of conventions. For general information on Chinese, Muslim, and Indian naming conventions, please see Appendix A.
- The Sinhalese will generally have two names, the first one indicating a house, tribe, profession, or other important family characteristic. This name sometimes has a *GE* written after it. This is followed by a person's given or first name.
- Tamils also have two main names. The father's comes first, then the child's. Many people (both Tamils and Sinhalese) use an initial for their first names.
- It is best to ask someone how he or she prefers to be addressed.

Gestures

- The left hand is taboo for most purposes, because it was historically used for hygienic purposes. Therefore, do not use this hand when eating, passing food or objects, or touching another person.
- Nonverbal signals for agreement are reversed from those in Western countries. A nod of the head may mean "no," and shaking your head from side to side can indicate "yes."
- Pointing with your finger is considered rude. Beckon a person by waving your fingers with the hand extended, palm down.
- Smiling can be considered flirtatious.
- The head is considered sacred, and the feet are dirty. Therefore, do not touch another's head and do not prop your feet up on desks or chairs.

Gifts

- If you are invited to a home for a meal, a gift is not expected but will be appreciated.
- Good gifts include fruit, imported chocolates, and crafts from home.
- Before giving liquor, be certain that the recipient drinks alcohol; if so, then a bottle of imported whiskey would be a good choice.

Dress

- Business dress is usually conservative, but lightweight, in consideration of the climate. Men should wear a light shirt and pants. Jackets and ties are rarely worn. Women should wear a modest, light blouse and skirt. Your Sri Lankan counterpart will probably dress conservatively.
- Nice, yet cool clothing is appropriate for casualwear. Shorts, low-cut, revealing, or sleeveless clothing and bathing suits are inappropriate for women except in resort areas or on the beach. Western dress is common among younger Sri Lankans.

Taiwan

Republic of China
Local short form: T'ai-wan
Local long form: Chung-hua min-k'uo
Former: Formosa

Cultural Note

The Taiwanese are justifiably sensitive about their relationship with mainland China (the People's Republic of China). Even though their economies are intricately interconnected, the PRC continues to issue threatening statements regarding the inadvisability of the "secession of Taiwan." Despite these declarations, the Taiwanese continue to hold onto their views on national identity.

▶ WHAT'S YOUR CULTURAL IQ?

1. Studies show that Asians sleep fewer hours each night than North Americans and Europeans. In Taipei, many businesses stay open twenty-four hours a day. Which of the following firms cater to Taipei's night owls?
   a. Florists
   b. Internet cafés
   c. Opticians
   d. Bookstores
   e. All of the above
   ANSWER: e. Residents of Taipei shop all night long.

2. In 1999, an earthquake measuring 7.6 on the Richter scale struck Taiwan. Over 2,000 people died, nearly 9,000 were injured, and approximately 10,000 were homeless. Which relief organization was most effective in immediately getting aid to the survivors?

    a. The Red Cross

    b. The Tzu-Chi Foundation

    c. The World Health Organization

ANSWER: b. Tzu-Chi is led by a Buddhist nun, Dharma Master Cheng Yen. She mobilized hundreds of Tzu Chi volunteers immediately after the quake, long before other relief efforts arrived—because Tzu Chi volunteers were part of each neighborhood.

3. Taiwan's citizens are keenly competitive, and they look worldwide for new clients. The most common type of company in Taiwan is:

    a. A massive corporation with global reach

    b. A small family-run company

    c. A venture capital firm

ANSWER: b. While there are immense multinationals in Taiwan (which have done immense damage to the environment), the archetype company is the flexible, entrepreneurial enterprise.

◉ TIPS ON DOING BUSINESS IN TAIWAN

- The Taiwanese are a fairly small and slender people. The large size of average Westerners can be intimidating. If you can find a way to compensate for this difference (such as sitting down, or standing on a lower level, so you and your Taiwanese counterpart are at comparable heights), do so. Also, large Westerners should realize that everything from furniture to clothing is made to a smaller scale in Taiwan.

- Western men who wear beards can be at a disadvantage. Taiwanese men are usually clean-shaven except after the death of their father or brother (they stay unshaven during the traditional seven-week mourning period). In fact, one of the Taiwanese terms for foreigners is *ang mo*, meaning red beard. The term can be used for bearded or clean-shaven foreigners of any hair color, and is not complimentary. It plays into the stereotype of Westerners as hairy, unkempt barbarians. Westerners can fight this characterization by being beardless and well groomed.

- Executives in the health care and medical supply industries must face the Taiwanese reluctance to discuss illness. People in Taiwan do not even like to give health warnings, nor do they comment on illness to a sick person. The insurance industry has gotten around this reluctance by speaking of insurance as if it were a bet (many Taiwanese love gambling). A life insurance salesperson will explain a policy by saying, "We will bet that you will live to age sixty, and if we lose, we will pay your beneficiaries."

- While nepotism is a fact of life in Taiwan, foreign companies might not want to hire multiple members of the same family. Since loyalty to the family is one of the basic tenets of Taiwanese life, when you have several family members working in one office they may begin to work for their family's interest rather than the company's.

- Although Taiwan does not have any official cultural and commercial relations with various countries, (including the United States of America), they may have specific offices that maintain unofficial diplomatic representation. In the United States, the Taipei Economic and Cultural Representative Office *(www.tecro.org)* has offices in Washington, DC, and other cities. Concomitantly, many countries maintain unofficial relations through their offices in Taiwan, like the American Institute in Taiwan (AIT) and the American Trade Center—both in Taipei. Further Taiwanese governmental information is available at *www.roc-taiwan.org*.

▶ COUNTRY BACKGROUND

Demographics
Taiwan's population of 23 million (2006 estimate) is primarily Taiwanese and mainland Chinese. Only 2 percent of the population consists of the aboriginal inhabitants of Taiwan. Although they live together amicably, there is some tension between the groups.

History
Migration to Taiwan from mainland China began in A.D. 500. Dutch traders claimed the island as a base for their trade in 1624 and administered it until 1661. In 1664, loyalists from the Ming dynasty fled to Taiwan to escape the Manchu invasion, and in 1683

it came under Manchurian control. When Taiwan became a Chinese province three years later, migration increased to the point where the Chinese dominated the aboriginal population. In 1895, following the first Sino-Japanese war, Taiwan was annexed to Japan. During the next fifty years, Taiwan underwent agricultural development and the construction of a modern transportation network. At the end of World War II, Taiwan again became governed by China.

A revolution founded the Republic of China (ROC) under Sun Yat-sen's Kuomintang (KMT) Party. However, a civil war was waged in China between the KMT forces (led by Chiang Kai-shek after the death of Sun in 1925) and the Communist forces of Mao Tse-tung. The KMT was defeated, and the refugees fled to Taiwan. The provisional government they established claimed to be the only legitimate government over both the mainland and Taiwan.

Many countries supported Taiwan as the legitimate government until 1971, when the People's Republic of China was admitted to the United Nations in place of the Republic of China. The United States of America opened relations with the mainland government in 1979.

A peaceful solution to the Chinese situation is still being sought. Debate continues over Taiwan becoming a separate, independent country. More recently, hope has arisen that the PRC will democratize to the extent that reunification may occur.

After his death in 1975, Chiang Kai-shek was succeeded by his son Chiang Ching-kuo. Extensive modernization efforts created a growing and prosperous economy in Taiwan. Martial law was lifted in 1987, and political opposition was legalized in 1989, opening the way for multiparty democratic elections.

Relations with Japan, the USA, and other countries are good, and extensive trading continues.

Cultural Note

Modernization has come swiftly to Taiwan, making it one of the wealthiest countries in East Asia. Fast-food restaurants, the latest high-tech gadgets, and luxury items are evident. This is attributed in part to the long-term stability of the government and strong feelings of solidarity and nationalism. The Taiwanese are generally quiet and reserved, yet friendly and courteous to strangers.

Type of Government

The nation's official name is Republic of China. It is often known as Nationalist China. After years as a one-party presidential regime, Taiwan is now a multiparty republic. Political opposition parties were legalized in 1989.

Taiwan's constitutional system divides the government into five branches, or Yuans. They are: the Executive Yuan, the Legislative, the Judicial, a Control Yuan that monitors public service and corruption, and the Examination Yuan that serves as a civil service commission. At the top of this structure is the chief of state, the president, who is chosen by the National Assembly. The head of government is the Premier, who is appointed by the president.

Taiwan held its first popular election for president in March of 1996. Since the People's Republic of China remains a one-party state, the Taiwanese election of 1996 was the first time in 4,000 years of recorded history that a Chinese nation held a free and fair election.

The KMT, which brought its political power and 2 million people over from Mainland China in 1949, was historically associated with the Mainlanders (i.e., people who fled to Taiwan with the KMT and their descendants).

For the first time, a member of the main opposition party, the Democratic Progressive Party (DPP), was elected in 2004. President Chen Shui-bian succeeded the KMT's Mr. Lee Teng-hui. The DP Party's most salient policy difference with the KMT has been the controversial issue of Taiwan's independence. The DPP modified its demand for immediate Taiwan independence and now calls for the people to decide Taiwan's future through a plebiscite. The DPP has also staked out generally populist positions of concern for the environment and for working people.

The third-largest opposition party is the Chinese New Party, which consists mainly of second-generation "mainlanders" who have grown up in Taiwan. The New Party supports the eventual reintegration of Taiwan into the People's Republic of China.

The defining characteristic of Taiwan's international presence is its lack of diplomatic ties with most nations of the world. The ruling authorities in Taiwan call their administration the "Republic of

China," and for many years claimed to be the legitimate government of all China. Foreign nations wishing to establish diplomatic relations with a government of China had two choices: to recognize the "Republic of China" or to recognize the People's Republic of China (PRC). Most chose to recognize the PRC. The PRC was admitted to—and Taiwan left—the United Nations and most related organizations in the early seventies. The United States of America switched diplomatic recognition to the PRC in 1979. Taiwan's authorities backed away from their stance of insisting that they are the legitimate rulers of all of China years ago. While still admitting that Taiwan is part of China, they now seek recognition as one of two "legitimate political entities" in China, the other being the PRC. Under this policy, Taiwan seeks to join various international organizations, including the United Nations. Taiwan has been able to join the Asia-Pacific Cooperation (APEC) dialogue as an "economy" and other entities as a "customs territory." Current government data can be found at the Embassy of Taiwan at *www.roc-taiwan.org.*

Cultural Note

Although Taiwan initially used only the old forms of written Chinese, they eventually adopted some (but not all) of the improved, simplified Chinese characters developed by the Communists. Visiting executives should make sure the Taiwanese variant is used for translations of their materials in Taiwan.

Westerners who wish to speak Chinese should be thankful that Mandarin was chosen as Taiwan's official language. Mandarin, with four different tones, is difficult enough to learn. The native Taiwanese language (imported from southern Fukien province) has six tones, which change depending upon the position of a word in the sentence!

Language

The official language of Taiwan is traditional Mandarin Chinese, although Taiwanese (called "Min," a southern Fukien dialect), and Hakka dialects are spoken. English is a popular language to study in school, and many businesspeople can speak, understand, and correspond in English. In general, Taiwan uses the Wade-Giles system for romanization, but the special municipality of Taipei adopted standard

Pinyin romanization for street and place names. This means that the same Chinese word may be transcribed various ways into English.

For further data on the languages of Taiwan, see Ethnologue at *www.ethnologue.com.*

Cultural Note

The Chinese phrase that describes so much of Taiwanese life is *re nau,* which means "hot and raucous." This describes not just Taiwan's lively nightlife, but the aggressive nature of daytime Taiwan as well. The streets and the noise are overwhelming; everyone has something to do and is in a hurry. It is this energy that developed Taiwan into a major industrial power in half a century.

The Taiwanese View

The religious distribution is over 90 percent Buddhist, Confucian, and Taoist; 4.5 percent Christian; and 2.5 percent other religions.

A Taiwanese citizen does not have to wonder about the meaning of life. The Mandarin term *shengyi* translates as "meaning of life." It also means "business." There could be no greater work ethic than this: the purpose of life in Taiwan is to work hard, be successful in business, and accumulate wealth for one's family.

Confucian ethics form the backbone of Taiwan society. Confucianism is not a religion in the Western sense, but it does provide guides for living. Unlike the People's Republic of China (where the Communists preached loyalty to one's work group), in Taiwan the family remains the central unit of society.

Taiwan has no official religion, reflecting the ability of the Taiwanese to simultaneously follow more than one religion. Aside from Confucianism and traditional folk beliefs, Taiwanese are likely to be Buddhist, Taoist, or Christian. (To make matters more complicated, many Taiwanese follow Taoist philosophy while ignoring the Taoist priesthood.)

Cultural Note

Business travelers to Taiwan should refer to the People's Republic of China as "mainland China" and to Beijing as "Peking" or "Beiping," which means "northern peace" rather than "northern capital."

☑ Know Before You Go

Taiwan sits in the Pacific's "Ring of Fire"—right above the juncture of the Philippine and Eurasian plates—in a seismically volatile region (as evidenced by the earthquake in September of 1999). Some geologists believe that Taiwan is ultimately doomed. Still, it is such an economic powerhouse that the risks are far outweighed by the monetary rewards of establishing facilities on the island. A similar situation exists in many parts of the U.S West Coast. Earthquakes, typhoons, heavy air pollution, and contaminated drinking water are all hazards that Taiwanese face. Besides being continually cloudy most of the year, the monsoons generally hit Taiwan from June to August.

▶ CULTURAL ORIENTATION

Cognitive Styles: How the Taiwanese Organize and Process Information

Taiwan's culture is generally closed to outside information but willing to consider data that conforms to its vital interests. Taiwanese are trained to think associatively and to stress wholeness over fragmentation. They are more apt to let their personal involvement in a problem dictate its solution than to use rules or laws.

Negotiation Strategies: What the Taiwanese Accept as Evidence

One's immediate feelings are the primary source of truth. This may be biased by faith in the ideologies of nationalism. Recently, younger Taiwanese are moving toward the use of more and more facts to justify their decisions.

Value Systems: The Basis for Behavior

Confucianism has a great influence on Chinese society. It generates a rigid ethical and moral system that governs all relationships. The following three sections identify the Value Systems in the predominant culture—their methods of dividing right from wrong, good from evil, and so forth.

Locus of Decision-Making

Decisions are made by consensus of the group, which defers to those who have the most ethos—usually the oldest members. It is the individual's duty not to bring shame on any unit of which he or she is a member—family, group, or organization. Individuals must also be very careful not to cause someone else to lose face. Thus, Taiwanese may speak with vague politeness rather than saying "no." There is a strong authoritative structure that demands impartiality and obedience.

Sources of Anxiety Reduction

The family is the most important unit of social organization, and life is an organization of obligations to relationships. The Taiwanese are highly ethnocentric with a natural feeling of superiority and confidence in their political system. This gives them a feeling of national and personal security. One must work for harmony in the group, so emotional restraint is prized and aggressive behavior is frowned upon.

Issues of Equality/Inequality

There is a strong feeling of interdependence among members of the family, group, or organization. Businesses are very competitive and put heavy emphasis on entry-level skills and one's ability to get along in the group. Taiwan is still a male-dominated society with clearly differentiated sex roles. There is a strong women's movement.

⊚ BUSINESS PRACTICES

Punctuality, Appointments, and Local Time

- Business hours are generally 8:30 A.M. to noon and 1:00 to 5:00 P.M., Monday through Friday, and 8:30 A.M. to noon on Saturday.
- Foreigners are expected to be punctual to meetings. Do not get upset, however, if your counterpart is late.
- Evening entertainment is an important part of doing business in Taiwan, so expect to be out late. It is wise to schedule morning appointments for late morning. This gives both you and your client a chance to rest.
- Plan a visit to Taiwan between April and September. Many businesspeople vacation from January through March.

- Traffic in Taipei is very congested. Unless your next appointment is so close that you can get there on foot, plan for long travel times between appointments.
- Taiwanese write the day first, then the month, and then the year (e.g., December 3, 2010, is written 3.12.10 or 3/12/10).
- For a list of official holidays in Taiwan, visit *www.kissboworshake hands.com.*
- Local time is eight hours ahead of Greenwich Mean Time (G.M.T. + 8) or thirteen hours ahead of U.S. Eastern Standard Time (E.S.T. + 13).

Cultural Note

Modesty is very important in Taiwan. Do not enter an office until you are invited, and do not seat yourself until you are asked to do so. If you receive a compliment, politely refute it and expect others to do the same. This should not stop you from complimenting another person, however, because compliments are always appreciated.

Negotiating

- The basis of a business relationship in Taiwan is respect and trust. Take time to establish a rapport with your counterpart. Initially, you will have to overcome the Taiwanese distrust of Westerners. Meet face-to-face as often as possible, and keep in touch after your trip is over.
- Taiwan is relatively similar to other East Asian countries. The Chinese in Taiwan are capitalists with the same motivations for doing business as the Japanese. However, while Taiwan may seem very westernized, the heart of the culture is still very traditional.
- Business will tend to take place at a slower pace than in North America or Europe. Be patient with delays. Often, this is a tactic to wear down the other side. Therefore, do not talk about your deadlines. Expect to make several trips before reaching an agreement.
- Your negotiating team should include persons with seniority and a thorough knowledge of your company. Most importantly, include an older person. The Chinese revere age and status—sending a

senior executive shows that a company is serious about starting a business relationship.

- Brute honesty is not appreciated in Taiwan. A direct "no" is considered rude. Learn to speak in and listen to subtleties. A "yes" or nod of the head may mean "maybe" or "I understand." A "maybe" usually means "no."

- When negotiating, be sincere and honest. Humility is a virtue, and a breach of trust, since trust is a vital factor in business relationships, will not be taken lightly. (Most proposals and potential business partners will be thoroughly investigated.)

- Emphasize the compatibility of your two firms, your personal amicability, and your desire to work with your counterpart. Profits are very important, but harmonious human interaction precedes them in importance. Avoid high-pressure tactics.

- Saving "face" or individual dignity is a very important and delicate matter. Therefore, never embarrass another person, especially in public.

- Never criticize your competition or avoid admitting that you do not know the answer to a question.

- Consider sending your proposals in advance of your visit for your host to preview. At a presentation, recap the major points at the beginning and at the end. Look for cues that your counterpart did not understand you. Do not expect him or her to tell you when this happens, because this will be embarrassing. Break up the information into small segments with pauses for question-and-answer periods. Be patient with extensive questioning. Address the chief negotiator occasionally, even if he does not speak English.

- Avoid using your hands when speaking. Chinese rarely use their hands while speaking and become distracted by a speaker who does.

- Business is competitive in Taiwan. Be prepared to discuss all parts of your proposal in detail. Bargaining is also a way of life, so be prepared to make concessions.

- Be sure to have products patented or registered in Taiwan to protect yourself against imitation.

- Have written materials translated by a Taiwanese expert. It is not acceptable to use the simplified Chinese script used in the People's Republic of China.
- Treat the elderly with respect. Acknowledge them first in a group, and do not smoke or wear sunglasses when they are near. When going through a doorway, allow older people to pass first. If they refuse, gently insist upon this point of etiquette.
- Try to obtain a personal introduction, possibly through your bank or government's Department of International Trade, since local contacts are extremely important.
- Be prepared to give out a lot of business cards. Your name, company, and title should be printed in English on one side and in Mandarin Chinese on the reverse side. (Gold ink is the most prestigious color for the Chinese side.) Cards are very important, because they indicate your rank and are a key to the respect you deserve in their culture. Never place a person's card in your wallet and then put it in your back pocket.
- For meetings, you will probably be taken to an informal sitting area and served coffee and tea. At the table, the member of your team with the highest seniority should sit in the middle of one long side. The second-ranked person will sit at his right, the third-ranked person to his left, and so forth. The Chinese delegation will do the same, so you will be able to identify key players on their team. If you are sitting on a sofa and chairs, follow the same pattern.
- Important issues to be aware of include observing hierarchy, respecting the elderly, modesty, and reciprocating gestures of goodwill.

Business Entertaining
- Hospitality is very, very important. Expect to be invited out every night after hours. This will entail visiting local nightspots and clubs, often until late at night.
- Be careful not to overly admire an object belonging to another person. He or she may feel obliged to give it to you.
- Remove your shoes when entering a home or a temple building.

- Do not be surprised if you are asked personal questions. You may be asked how much you paid for something, or what your salary is. These questions are not considered in bad taste in Taiwan.
- The largest meal of the day is in the evening, around 6:00 P.M. Entertaining is most often done in a restaurant and rarely in a home. If you are invited to a home, consider this an honor. Do not discuss business during a meal unless your host brings it up first.
- Never visit a home unannounced. Before leaving, express your thanks and bow slightly. Send a thank-you note to your host after a meal. It is polite to reciprocate by inviting your host to a meal of equal value at a later date.
- If you are the guest of honor at a round table, you will be seated facing the door. This is a custom carried over from feudal times that signified trust and goodwill on the part of the host, as the guest would be the first to see an attack and the host would be the last.
- At a meal, eat lightly in the beginning, because there could be up to twenty courses served. Expect your host to keep filling your bowl with food whenever you empty it. Finishing all of your food is an insult to your host, because it means that he did not provide enough and that you are still hungry. Leaving a full bowl is also rude. The trick is to leave an amount somewhere in the middle.
- Chinese use chopsticks for eating and a porcelain spoon for soup. Your attempts at using chopsticks will be appreciated. When you are finished, set your chopsticks on the table or on the rest. Placing them parallel on top of your bowl is considered a sign of bad luck.
- Sticking your chopsticks straight up in your rice bowl is rude, as they will resemble the joss sticks used in religious ceremonies. Hold your rice bowl near your mouth to eat.
- Do not put food taken from a serving dish directly into your mouth. Transfer it to your plate or bowl first. Bones and shells are placed on the table or a spare plate; they are never placed in your rice bowl or on your plate.
- Leave promptly after the meal is finished.
- Good topics of conversation include Chinese sights, art, calligraphy, family, and inquiries about the health of the other's family.

Topics to avoid are the situation with mainland China and local politics. Generally, conversation during a meal focuses on the meal itself and is full of compliments to the preparer.

▶ PROTOCOL

Greetings
- With younger or foreign-educated Taiwanese, a handshake is the most common form of greeting. The standard Asian handshake is more of a handclasp; it is gentle and lasts for some ten or twelve seconds. (By contrast, most North American handshakes last for only three or four seconds.) Sometimes both hands will be used.
- When meeting someone for the first time, a nod of the head may be sufficient. When meeting friends or acquaintances, a handshake is appropriate and will be expected from Westerners. Show respect by bowing slightly with your hands at your sides and your feet together.
- Chinese women shake hands more often these days. Western women may have to initiate a handshake with Chinese men.
- Elderly people are highly respected, so it is polite to speak with them first. A compliment on their good health is always appreciated.
- Don't be surprised if you are asked if you have eaten. This is a common greeting, originating during the famines of feudal times. This phrase is comparable with "How are you?" in the West. A polite response is "yes," even if you have not eaten.
- Wait to be introduced to another at gatherings and parties. Avoid introducing yourself. Instead, employ a third person if there is someone you wish to meet.

Titles/Forms of Address
- A notable aspect of Taiwan is that, when they work with foreigners, they will list their names in the same order as Westerners. The given name (or two hyphenated names) comes first, and their family (or surname) is last.
- Foreign executives may also notice that Taiwanese businesspeople will usually have an English first name, which they use constantly

with English speakers. These English names (Sue, Tony, etc.) are often selected or assigned in school—and many Taiwanese just keep them for work purposes.

- If you require a Taiwanese businessperson to sign a document, he or she will probably use the Chinese version of his or her name. (When they sign, their names may be listed in traditional Chinese order—last name followed by two hyphenated given names.)
- For further information on Chinese naming conventions, please see Appendix A.

Gestures

- Do not wink at a person, even in friendship.
- Do not put your arm around another's shoulders. While young children of the same sex will often hold hands, it is inappropriate for others to do so or to make physical contact with people who are not good friends or family.
- Do not touch the head of another person's child. Children are considered precious, and it is believed that they may be damaged by careless touching.
- Feet are considered dirty and should not touch things or people. Men should keep their feet flat on the floor, while women are permitted to cross their legs.
- Chinese point with their open hands, because pointing with a finger is considered rude. They beckon by extending their arms palm down and waving their fingers.
- While Westerners point to their chests to indicate the first person, "I," Chinese will point to their noses to indicate the same thing.

Gifts

- Gift giving is often practiced within a business setting. Good gifts for a first trip include items with small company logos on them. Be sure and check that the products were manufactured in your home country.
- Other popular gifts to business people include imported liquor, gold pens, and magazine subscriptions focused on your Chinese associate's hobbies or interests.

- When giving or receiving a gift, use both hands. The gift is not opened in the presence of the giver.
- The Chinese traditionally decline a gift three times before accepting; this prevents them from appearing greedy. Continue to insist; once they accept the gift, say that you are pleased that they have done so.
- Gifts of food are always appreciated, but avoid bringing food gifts with you to a dinner or party (unless it has been agreed upon beforehand). To bring food may imply that your host cannot provide enough. Instead, send food as a thank-you gift afterward. Candy or fruit baskets are good choices.
- The list of inappropriate and appropriate gifts in the chapter on the People's Republic of China can be applied to Taiwan as well.

Dress
- For business, men should wear a conservative suit and tie. A jacket may be removed during meetings if your Chinese counterpart does so first. Women should wear a conservative skirt and blouse or suit.
- Dress modestly for casual activities.
- Revealing clothing for women is considered a mark of poor character.
- Shorts are appropriate for young people.
- Neatness and cleanliness are important.

Cultural Note
Avoid being loud and boisterous around the Taiwanese. They sometimes interpret strong emotions, either positive or negative, as a loss of self-control. Westerners can be stereotyped in Taiwan as being raucous and emotional. Eschew lurid or gaudy attire as well.

Thailand

Kingdom of Thailand
Former: Siam

Cultural Note

Thailand is the only country in Southeast Asia never to have been a European colony. The country consistently remained free of European rule (a point of great national pride to the Thais). Thailand signed trade treaties with both France and Britain under the rule of King Mongkut and his son, King Chulalongkorn. By playing France and England off against each other, the Thai kings kept their country free. The name "Thai" means "free."

▶ WHAT'S YOUR CULTURAL IQ?

1. A *wai* is:
   a. A spicy dish made with peppers and rice
   b. An inquiry
   c. A form of greeting
   ANSWER: c. A wai is the beautiful Thai greeting which is a combination of hands pressed together and a slight bow. Foreigners are not generally expected to know how to perform it correctly—but an attempt is appreciated.

2. Many of Thailand's cities celebrate *Songkran*, which is a Sanskrit word that refers to the orbit of the sun moving into Aries. It marks the beginning of a new solar year—the Thai New Year. TRUE or FALSE: The celebrations usually involve throwing water on people.
   ANSWER: TRUE. From sprinkling water on statues of Buddha, to (politely!) dousing friends with buckets of water, Thais enthusiastically celebrate Songkran over several days in April. It is a cleansing, purifying holiday that Thais use to mark a new beginning, start fresh, and to give thanks.

3. Thailand's currency is the:
   a. baht
   b. dong
   c. rupee

   ANSWER: a. The baht's currency code is THB. (Vietnam uses the dong, and Nepal and India use the rupee)

▶ TIPS ON DOING BUSINESS IN THAILAND

- Thailand advertises itself as "The Land of Smiles," and the Thai people are genuinely friendly and polite. But their extreme politeness vanishes as soon as they get behind the wheel of a car. Driving is aggressive, and pedestrians seem to be fair game. Be very cautious every time you cross a street; use an overhead walkway if possible.

- Because of travel difficulties in large Thai cities, many foreign executives plan on making only two meetings per day. The gridlock in Bangkok is so bad that many Thai businesspeople conduct business from their cars, with cell phones, laptops, and fax machines. (Remember that Bangkok and other Thai cities have passenger service on canals. When the street traffic is stalled, consider commuting by boat.)

- English is often spoken by Thai executives. For those who do not speak English, a translator is usually close at hand. Note that taxi drivers do not usually speak English. To arrive at your destination, have the street address written down in Thai, plus the name of the nearest major cross street.

- Entertaining is part of developing business relationships. Thais place great value on enjoyment *(kwam sanuk)*. Laughter comes easily to Thais, and a foreigner can minimize his or her inevitable errors by laughing at them. Laughter can also be used to cover embarrassment.

- Giving gifts will help create a good first impression. A bottle of imported liquor (such as single malt Scotch) is appropriate for an executive. Have the gift-wrapped locally, and do not be dismayed if the gift is immediately set aside—Thais do not open gifts in the presence of the giver. Some executives recommend giving a small gift to the office receptionist or secretary as well, like food or candy that can be shared with the rest of the office staff.

⊙ COUNTRY BACKGROUND

Demographics
Thailand has a population of about 65 million (2006 estimate). Approximately 10 percent of the population lives in Bangkok, the country's capital and largest city. About 75 percent of the people are ethnic Thais, 14 percent are Chinese, and the remaining 11 percent are a mixture of other Asians and non-Asians.

History
Like other countries of Southeast Asia, Thailand was peopled in prehistoric times through successive migrations from central Asia. Evidence of Bronze Age civilizations in northeast Thailand illustrate a high level of technology achieved by prehistoric people in Southeast Asia.

During the eleventh century, the Thai people began migrating from southern China. (Some research indicates that they were forced out by the Han Chinese.)

From the thirteenth century to the early twentieth century, the country was called Siam. The name was changed to Thailand in 1939.

Thailand was ruled by an absolute monarchy until a group of foreign-educated Thais directed a military and civilian coup d'etat in June of 1932 and replaced the absolute monarchy with a constitutional monarchy. The current nation can be dated to that period.

In 1941 Japan occupied Thailand. After World War II, Thailand followed a pro-Western foreign policy.

Since the Second World War, a balance of power has been established between the military and the civilian leaders, with the king occasionally mediating. Whenever the military has felt threatened, it seized power. This has become more difficult as a growing political consciousness has developed in the Thai people. The Thais hope that the days of military coups are now over.

In 2005 Dr. Thaksin's Thai Rak Thai Party was re-elected, winning Thailand's parliamentary election with an overwhelming majority. One major challenge he faced was an insurgency of Muslims in the southern provinces.

His viewpoint on resolving the conflict was to reduce government funds and increase military force in the separatists' villages. Dissatisfaction with Thaksin's policies led to the ouster of his government by a military-led coup in September 2006.

Type of Government

The Kingdom of Thailand is a constitutional monarchy.

Thailand has a prime minister and a parliament with two legislative houses, but their power has been limited by the military. Membership in the lower house is by election, but in the upper house it is by appointment, and the military is well represented. As of this writing it is uncertain how Thailand's form of government will be affected by the military coup of September 2006.

Current government data can be found at the Embassy of Thailand at *www.thaiembdc.org.*

Language

Thai, which is linguistically related to Chinese, is the official language. Other languages are spoken, including Chinese, Lao, Khmer, and Malay. The literacy rate is 89 percent.

Cultural Note

Thai is a complex language with five different tones. While this makes it difficult for Westerners to speak, Thais will appreciate a foreigner who takes the time to learn even a few phrases in Thai. There are only eight possible consonants that a word in Thai may end with: *p, t, k, m, n, ng, w,* and *y.* Consequently, when Thais speak English, they have trouble with words that end in other sounds. English words ending in *l* tend to be shifted to the *n* sound; for example, the word "Oriental Hotel" is pronounced "Orienten Hoten." And, because the *s* sound is not used in endings, Thais tend to leave the *s* off of pluralized words. The Thai alphabet is similar to the alphabets used in Burmese and Laotian scripts. Thai is written from left to right. Adding to the difficulty for Westerners, there are no spaces between individual words.

The Thai alphabet is completely different from the Roman alphabet, and there are multiple ways to transliterate words, therefore, Thai words may be spelled different ways in English.

Ethnologue.com lists the number of languages in Thailand as seventy-five.

The Thai View

About 95 percent of Thais follow the Theravada form of Buddhism (an early form of Buddhism). About 4 percent of the population is Muslims, with the remaining split between other religions (including Christianity).

Adherents to the Theravada school consider themselves followers of the form closest to Buddhism as it was originally practiced. The spiritual liberation of the individual is a main focus of the Theravada school. Each individual is considered responsible for his or her own actions and destiny.

Each person in Thai society has a specific place. It is every person's job to fulfill his or her role with a minimum of fuss. Failure to do so involve a loss of personal dignity (called a loss of face). The Thai phrase *"mai pen rai"* (meaning "never mind" or "no worries") is frequently invoked as a reminder not to risk opposing the unopposable.

☑ Know Before You Go

If you are trying to keep correspondence private, it is probably not advisable to mark it "Confidential." Thai culture would consider that almost a teaser, which would bring it more attention than you wish.

The water table has been depleted in Bangkok, and the area now must deal with subsidence. Thais also face droughts, air, and water pollution, and the catastrophic effects of the 2004 tsunami.

▶ CULTURAL ORIENTATION

Cognitive Styles: How Thais Organize and Process Information

Thais cultivate alternatives and are usually open to information on most issues. They live in a concrete, associative, pragmatic world where the present is more important than the future and the person takes precedence over the rule or law.

Negotiation Strategies: What Thais Accept as Evidence

The truth develops from subjective, fatalistic feelings on the issue modified by faith in the ideologies of Theravada Buddhism. Thais with higher education from foreign universities may accept objective facts as a sole basis for evidence.

Value Systems: The Basis for Behavior

Religion plays a very important part in a Thai's life, but it does not dictate his or her every move. There are no absolute demands because their form of Buddhism permits selective conformity. They are free to choose which precepts of Buddhism, if any, they will follow.

Locus of Decision-Making

The individual is responsible for his or her decisions. Thais are nonassertive, as well as being very conscious of the feelings of others and their position in the social hierarchy. Decision-making revolves around the hierarchical, centralized nature of authority and the dependence of the subordinate upon the superior. Thus, the typical supervisor is authoritarian. He or she makes decisions autonomously, and the inferior unquestioningly obeys.

A benevolent superior and a respectful subordinate is the Thai ideal.

Sources of Anxiety Reduction

The extended family is the basic social unit, with structure provided by the family, the village, and the *wat* (temple). The king is the primary provider of social cohesiveness. Thais refrain from developing specific expectations whenever possible because fate and luck play a major role in any event. You cannot plan because you cannot predict, so Thais live with a great deal of uncertainty. There is a high sense of self-reliance—what a person is depends on his or her own initiative.

Issues of Equality/Inequality

Status is of primary importance, as hierarchical relations are at the heart of Thai society. However, people gain their social position as a result of karma, not personal achievement. The royal family and the nobility are the only real class-conscious segment, although a class-conscious society is emerging. Regional and ethnic differences are socially and politically significant. This is a male-dominated society.

▶ BUSINESS PRACTICES

Punctuality, Appointments, and Local Time

- Business hours are generally 8:30 A.M. to 5:00 P.M., Monday through Friday. Shops are usually open from 10:00 A.M. to 6:30 or 7:00 P.M., Monday through Saturday. Smaller shops open earlier and close later.

- Punctuality is a sign of courtesy. Foreigners are expected to be on time.

- Traffic is extremely heavy in Bangkok, and floods make travel even worse. Allow plenty of time between appointments, especially during the rainy season.

- The best time to schedule a visit to Thailand is between November and March. Most businesspeople vacation during April and May. Avoid the weeks before and after Christmas, and the month of April. Thailand's Water Festival (Songkran) is held in April, and businesses close for an entire week.

- Call and e-mail as far in advance is it is as possible for you to arrange appointments.

- Arrange for a letter of introduction, and try to have an intermediary.

- Thais write the day first, then the month, and then the year (e.g., December 3, 2010, is written 3.12.10 or 3/12/10).

- For a list of the official holidays in Thailand, visit *www.kissbowor shakehands.com.*

- The country of Thailand is seven hours ahead of Greenwich Mean Time (G.M.T. + 7), or twelve hours ahead of U.S. Eastern Standard Time (E.S.T. + 12).

Negotiating

- Your initial meeting with Thai businesspeople may be over lunch or drinks, so they can get to know you. However, do not expect to discuss business during lunch.
- Because of the Thai deference to rank and authority, requests and correspondence usually pass through many layers before reaching top management.
- Be flexible and patient in your business dealings. Recognize that Thais do not follow the same relentless work schedule that other cultures do. Allow sufficient time to reach your goal.
- Never lose control of your emotions, and do not be overly assertive; that is considered poor manners.
- Thais avoid confrontation at all costs. They will never say "no," but will instead make implausible excuses or pretend that they don't understand English. They may even tell you that they must check with someone at a higher level, when such a person doesn't exist. Likewise, they find it difficult to accept a direct negative answer.
- Always present your business card, preferably with a translation printed in Thai on the opposite side. (You can have these printed in Bangkok.)
- Thai businesspeople will be impressed if you learn even a few words of Thai.
- If someone begins laughing for no apparent reason in a business meeting, change the subject. He or she is embarrassed.

Cultural Note

Direct confrontation is considered impolite. Do not ask questions that require a value judgment (for example, "Which of these competing products is the best?"). Use subtle questions, and work your way toward the answer ("Which of these competing products do you use?"). Don't make assumptions about the answer (for example, "So you use this one because it is best?" will probably elicit a "yes," even if the true reason is because a relative sells that brand).

Business Entertaining

- Never finish the last bit of food in a serving dish. Wait until it is offered to you and then refuse politely the first time. When it is offered again, accept; it is considered an honor to have the last bit of food.

- To entertain a small group, take them to an excellent restaurant in a prestigious hotel. For a large group, arrange a buffet supper. Always include Thai wives in business dinners.
- Expect to eat with Western-style forks and spoons. Keep the fork in the left hand and the spoon in the right (reverse this if you are left-handed). Cut with the side of the spoon, not the fork. Use the fork to push food onto the spoon.
- Drink tea or beer with meals. Drink water only if you have seen it being poured from a bottle.
- Many Thais smoke after dinner, but do not be the first to light up. Always pass cigarettes around to the men at the table. Although traditional Thai women do not smoke or drink in public, it is acceptable for Western women to do so.

Cultural Note

Monks are not permitted to touch the opposite sex. If you are female, do not expect them to shake your hand. If you need to give something to a monk, place it in front of him, or give it to a man to pass along. Monks are not expected to thank you for a contribution either—however, you always thank them for providing you with a means to better your life today, and in the future.

▶ PROTOCOL

Greetings

- The graceful, traditional Thai greeting is called a *wai*. Press your hands together as though in prayer, keeping arms and elbows close to your body, and bow your head to touch your fingers. The height of your hands is related to the level of deference or respect you are giving to the person you greet. The higher your hands, the more respect you show.
- A wai is used for both meeting and departing.
- Younger people are expected to greet an elder first, and they may or may not return the gesture.

- You do not have to wai children.
- Thais will shake hands with Westerners, but they will be pleased if you greet them with their traditional greeting.
- When introduced to a monk, never touch him; simply give a verbal greeting without shaking hands. Monks do not have to greet you with the wai.

Titles/Forms of Address
- Titles are very important.
- Many Thai businesspeople are Chinese.
- Chinese names generally consist of a family name, followed by two (sometimes one) personal names. In the name Chang Wu Jiang, "Chang" is the surname (or clan name). He would be addressed with his title plus Chang (Mr. Chang, Dr. Chang). For further information on the proper titles and forms of address for Chinese names, please see Appendix A.
- Ethnic Thais predominate in government positions, but they will also be found in the business world.
- Since the adoption of surnames in the 1920s, ethnic Thais generally have two names. Their given name will come first, then their surname. Given names in Thailand are often unique, and have a specific meaning. Only the most discerning travelers learn which ones apply to women and which to men.
- Address people by their title (or Mr./Mrs.) and their given (first) name. The short Thai term for "Mr.," "Mrs.," or "Miss" is Khun (although there are longer forms as well). Thus, former prime minister Chatichai Choonhavan could theoretically have been addressed as Khun Chatichai.
- Nicknames are popular in Thailand. Do not be surprised if the Thais give you a nickname, particularly if your name is hard for them to pronounce.

Gestures
- Public displays of affection between members of the opposite sex are not condoned. However, members of the same sex may touch or hold hands with one another.

- Never, ever point your foot at anyone; it is considered extremely rude. Don't cross your legs with one leg resting on the other knee, and never cross your legs in front of an older person.
- In contrast to the foot being foul, the head is sacred in Thailand. Never touch anyone on the head, not even a child.
- Do not pat people on the back or shoulders.
- Give up your seat on a bus or train to a monk who is standing.
- Never walk in front of Thais praying in a temple.
- Beckoning is done with the palm down and the fingers waved toward the body.

Gifts

- Gifts are not opened in the presence of the giver.
- If you are invited for a meal, bring flowers, cakes, or fruit. Don't bring marigolds or carnations, however, because they are associated with funerals.
- High-tech gadgets (MP3 players, etc.), local handicrafts from your home, finely made pens and stationery, imported perfumes, select liquors, cigarettes, and illustrated books from your area are all suitable gifts.

Cultural Note

Much has been written about Thailand's sex industry. Since the proliferation of HIV (approximately 600,000 Thais live with HIV or AIDS as of this writing), it is an even more perilous occupation—endangering providers and patrons alike. It is projected that 40,000 to 60,000 Thais will die from AIDS-related causes each year, the majority being between twenty and twenty-four years of age.

Dress

- For business, men should wear a lightweight suit or slacks and a jacket, white shirt and tie; women should wear plain, conservative dresses or suits. Women should not wear black dresses, a color the Thais reserve for funerals or mourning.
- Dress for success. Thais are impressed with a neat appearance and refined clothing.

- In casual settings, men should wear slacks and shirts, with or without ties; women should wear light dresses or skirts and blouses. Short-sleeved blouses are acceptable, but sleeveless ones are not. Both sexes may wear jeans (but may find them too hot). Shorts are acceptable on the streets, but not in the temples.
- Men should wear traditional summer formal attire for formal occasions—white jacket, black pants, and black tie; women should wear long dresses. Black is acceptable to wear at a formal event if it is accented with color.
- Be certain to wear modest clothing when you visit temples—no shorts. It is also advisable to wear old or inexpensive shoes when visiting temples. You must remove them before entering, and once in a while they may be stolen.
- Never wear rubber thongs on the street; they are considered very low class.

Cultural Note

Never make fun of the royal family; they are regarded as a strong unifying influence. Faced with a fractious Parliament and a strong military, the Thai people turn to their constitutional monarch for leadership. Visiting executives should only use the most respectful terms when referring to the king. There is no room for criticism or humor in reference to royals—unless you want serious repercussions. Some Thai citizens who have made negative comments about the royal family have been charged with *lèse majesté*, and jailed.

Vietnam

Socialist Republic of Vietnam
Local long form: Cong Hoa Xa Hoi Chu Nghia Viet Nam
Local short form: Viet Nam

Cultural Note

The process of transforming from a Communist command economy to a market-oriented economy is never easy. The government's lack of transparency and low pay to government officials is a recipe for corruption. Another problem is competition among government agencies for jurisdiction over foreign investments. At present, multiple bureaucracies may claim control over foreign-controlled business—and each of them want to impose licenses and taxes.

▶ WHAT'S YOUR CULTURAL IQ?

1. Vietnam was divided into two antagonistic countries between 1956 and 1975. TRUE or FALSE: During this time, the south was known as "The Democratic Republic of Vietnam," while the north chose the shorter "Republic of Vietnam."
ANSWER: FALSE. Reverse the names. South Vietnam used the name Republic of Vietnam. In common with other Communist-bloc countries, North Vietnam added "Democratic" to its name (although it was nothing of the sort).

2. The traditional Vietnamese coat of arms is decorated with four animals. TRUE or FALSE: Three of these animals on the coat of arms are mythological.
ANSWER: TRUE. The coat of arms boasts a dragon, a unicorn, a phoenix, and a turtle.

3. Match the following Vietnamese terms with the comestibles they represent:

a. Bia Hoi   1. Noodle soup
b. Nuoc Mam   2. Fresh beer (freshly brewed and served)
c. Pho   3. Rice wine
d. Ruou   4. Fish sauce

ANSWERS: a. 2; b. 4; c. 1; d. 3

▶ TIPS ON DOING BUSINESS IN VIETNAM

• The official governmental policy toward business in Vietnam is *doi moi* (renovation). While the execution may sometimes be rocky, there is official admission that changes must be made.

• The Communist government remains a major influence, corruption is common, and the infrastructure is still somewhat primitive. However, labor costs are extremely low and the Vietnamese are anxious for outside investments.

• Vietnam has more than a million eager, aggressive businesspeople. In addition to this motivated work force, Vietnam has a variety of natural resources. Besides exporting rice and other agricultural products, Vietnam has started exporting oil. Their recently developed oil reserves are producing tens of millions of barrels.

• Not long ago, there was only one five-star hotel in the entire nation of Vietnam: the venerable Sofitel Metropole in Ho Chi Min City (Saigon). By the late 1990s, several five-star hotels opened in both Ho Chi Min City and Hanoi. Today, there are ranges of accommodations that meet international standards.

• In common with other Confucian cultures, age is highly respected in Vietnam. Keep in mind that foreign business delegations should always include a senior member to whom the other members must defer in public. Similarly, foreigners must show great respect to the senior members of any Vietnamese organization. Older executives are viewed as more experienced, wiser, and should be held in esteem.

▶ COUNTRY BACKGROUND

Demographics

The current population of Vietnam is some 84 million (2006 estimate). As much as 90 percent of the population is considered ethnic Vietnamese. The largest minority has been the ethnic Chinese, who number more than 2 million. The third largest ethnic group is the ethnic Cambodians, who are known as the Khmer Krom. They live mostly near the border with Cambodia and number about 600,000.

History

Southeast Asia has been home to civilizations for thousands of years. China occupied the region for over 1,000 years, starting in 111 B.C. The region achieved independence from China in A.D. 939, and adopted a native dynasty of rulers. The ethnic Vietnamese were northerners who gradually moved south and eventually reached the Mekong delta.

The nation of Vietnam (as a country distinct from the rest of Southeast Asia) dates back only as far as the French colonization. The French began their conquest in 1858, and by 1885 they were in effective control of the entire country. The French allowed the Vietnamese emperors to remain on the throne, but they were subject to French orders.

By the start of the twentieth century, some French-educated Vietnamese began to agitate for independence. Ho Chi Minh, whom Vietnamese consider the father of Vietnamese independence, was one of these. Ho Chi Minh organized various groups into a nationalist front, although most anti-Communist groups refused to join.

Japan occupied Vietnam in the Second World War, demonstrating that the French could be defeated. At the end of the war, before the French could reassert power, Ho Chi Minh declared the birth of the independent Democratic Republic of Vietnam on 2 September 1945.

French forces returned and refused to acknowledge Vietnamese independence. An eight-year guerrilla war ensued. This ended with the defeat of the French and their anti-Communist Vietnamese allies at Dien Bien Phu in 1954. A peace conference convened in Geneva, Switzerland, resulting in the temporary division of Vietnam at approximately the seventeenth parallel. The Communists were given control of the north; the anti-Communists the south. The two halves of the country were intended to be reunited after a national election by July 1956. However, the anti-Communists refused to participate in the election. Consequently, the division of the country into North Vietnam and South Vietnam lasted for almost two decades.

North Vietnam, with the support of the USSR and the People's Republic of China, began another guerrilla war. With the French unwilling to commit troops, the United States of America decided to support South Vietnam. U.S. military forces were initially sent into combat in 1965 by President Johnson. The level of U.S. forces in Vietnam peaked at 534,000 in 1969. Widespread opposition to the war led politicians in Washington, DC, to attempt to replace U.S. troops with South Vietnamese forces. But the Army of South Vietnam was unable to stop the Communist forces, and Saigon, the South Vietnamese capital, fell on April 30, 1975. By the end of the year, both halves of the country were united under a Communist government as the Socialist Republic of Vietnam.

After consolidating its power after reunification, the government of Vietnam felt threatened by the Khmer Rouge in neighboring Cambodia. Vietnam invaded Cambodia in December 1978. While most Western governments did not approve of the Vietnamese government, they considered the genocidal Khmer Rouge the greater evil.

In 1989, Vietnam withdrew its troops from Cambodia, and by 1991, it had forged diplomatic relations with many countries, including China and the USA. Vietnam and the United States of America signed a trade accord in 1991, finally allowing Vietnamese goods into the USA.

Vietnam's national holiday is Vietnamese National Day, celebrated on the second of September. However, the most important holiday is always the three-day celebration for the lunar New Year, or Tet. For further official holidays, visit *www.kissboworshakehands.com*.

Type of Government

The Socialist Republic of Vietnam is a constitutional republic dominated by the Communist Party. The National Assembly is the supreme organ of the state. The president and prime minister of Vietnam are elected by the National Assembly. The president is the head of state. The prime minister can be described as head of the government, because he is charged with the day-to-day handling of government organizations.

The Vietnamese Communist Party holds a national congress every five years to formalize policies and to outline the country's overall direction. The Party Congress also elects a Central Committee, which usually meets at least twice a year.

For current government data, check with the Embassy of Vietnam at *www.vietnamembassy-usa.org*.

Cultural Note

Thanks to the influence of the French, Vietnamese is written in a modified Roman alphabet instead of Chinese ideographs.

Language

The official language is Vietnamese. English has now replaced French as the preferred second language.

Ethnologue.com has listed a total of 103 languages in Vietnam. Only one of these languages is extinct: a pidgin combining French and Vietnamese known as Tay Boi.

Cultural Note

Vietnam has two large religious groups (sometimes described as cults) that are unfamiliar to outsiders. Hoa Hao is derived from Buddhism, but advocates direct, simple worship without intermediaries. It was founded in 1939 by a man from the Mekong delta named Huynh Phu So. The French derided him as a "mad monk," and the political activities of his followers caused Hoa Hao to be banned periodically.

Cao Dai is even more unusual: it is a syncretic faith that combines aspects of all the religions of Vietnam. Created in the 1920s, its leader, Ngo Minh Chieu, mixed such diverse beliefs as ancestor worship, Buddhism, Christianity, and Islam. Cao Dai has a pantheon of unusual saints, including Joan of Arc, Victor Hugo, Louis Pasteur, and Napoleon Bonaparte!

The Vietnamese View

The constitution of the Socialist Republic of Vietnam guarantees freedom of religion. The country's diverse population follows many religious beliefs. Confucianism (which is a philosophy more than a religion) has had a great effect on Vietnamese thought and tradition. Historically, the largest and most important religion in Vietnam was Buddhism. Although the Communist government describes Buddhism as currently "in decline," it acknowledges that 70 percent of Vietnamese are "strongly influenced" by Buddhist tradition.

Many other religions are represented in Vietnam. Also, as is common in Asia, religious beliefs often overlap. Vietnamese Catholics also may go to Buddhist temples; Vietnamese Muslims also may engage in ancestor worship. The current breakdown of religion in Vietnam is:

Buddhist
Roman Catholic—10 percent (Catholicism entered Vietnam in the
    seventeenth century and was supported by the French colonials.)
Cao Dai—approximately 2 million
Hoa Hao—over 1 million
Protestant—less than a half-million
Islam—approximately 50,000 (Islam is concentrated among the
    Cham ethnic minority near the coastline in Central Vietnam.)

As you would expect, views on Vietnam vary between groups. Anti-Communists and supporters of the defeated South Vietnamese government view today's Vietnam rather critically. Many of these Vietnamese left around the time Saigon was overrun in 1975. The so-called "Boat People" who fled after the Communist absorption of all South Vietnam in 1976 may have cynical views of both Communist governments and the West, because many Boat People were left to languish in refugee camps for years by Western governments. (For example, some spent years in camps in British-ruled Hong Kong.)

Cultural Note

Avoid carrying proscribed drugs or narcotics into or out of Vietnam. As in Malaysia and Indonesia, drug smugglers are subject to the death penalty.

Finally, some of the many ethnic minorities of Vietnam may also dislike the Communist government. These include the Hmong, who were persecuted as allies of the USA, and Vietnam's ethnic Chinese—a traditional merchant class who were devastated when the Communists made private trade illegal in 1978. Almost a half-million ethnic Chinese left Vietnam during that period, primarily by boat. Many were encouraged to leave by the Vietnamese government. (This mistreatment of Vietnam's ethnic Chinese contributed to the attack on the Vietnamese border by the People's Republic of China in 1979.)

☑ Know Before You Go

To the average business traveler in Vietnam, the greatest hazard is vehicular traffic. Traffic in Vietnam's fast-growing cities is chaotic, with trucks, cars, motorcycles, and bicycles all competing for space. Pedestrians can be in as much danger as drivers and their passengers. Exercise caution and hire a driver rather than drive yourself.

After dark, foreigners should avoid using the less-regulated forms of transport, such as motorcycle taxis and cyclos (also known as pedicabs). Also, at any time of day, you should negotiate the fee before entering a motorcycle taxi or cyclo: they have no meters. In a taxi, insist your driver use his meter.

Violence against foreigners is very rare, in part because the penalties for harming a foreigner are draconian. A Vietnamese who killed a foreigner in 1996 was quickly found, tried, and executed.

Cultural Note

To date, Vietnam has had only one Nobel Prize laureate. In 1973, the Nobel Peace Prize was jointly awarded to Henry Kissinger and Le Duc Tho for their contributions to the Vietnamese peace negotiations. These were (to say the least) controversial choices—especially because the peace negotiations did not prevent North Vietnamese forces from overrunning South Vietnam in 1975–76. As it happened, Le Duc Tho declined to accept his peace prize.

▶ CULTURAL ORIENTATION

Vietnam's recent history has been highly dynamic and there has not been much detailed study of Vietnamese cultural orientations at the time of this publication. Pending further research, the following observations can be made:

Cognitive Styles: How Vietnamese Organize and Process Information

Historically, by accepting the foreign concept of Marxism, the leaders of Vietnam became closed to outside information. Because the Communist victory took the better part of a century, unswerving dedication to Marxist ideals became a necessity. However, the Communist reunification of divided Vietnam took place during the decline of global Communism. The dissolution of Vietnam's primary benefactor, the USSR, required the Vietnamese leadership to become more open to other, non-Communist ideals.

As a market-oriented society, Vietnam's decision makers and businesspeople have—of necessity—become more open to outside concepts and more analytic than associative. Nevertheless, they may place more value on relationships than obedience to abstract rules of behavior.

Negotiation Strategies: What Vietnamese Accept as Evidence

Vietnamese relate each instance to their own experience, making search for truth highly subjective. Even experienced Vietnamese businesspeople may not make decisions entirely based on objective facts.

Value Systems: The Basis for Behavior

The following three sections identify the Value Systems in the predominant culture—their methods of dividing right from wrong, good from evil, and so forth.

Locus of Decision-Making

While responsibility for decision-making rests on the shoulders of the individual, decisions are always made with the family in mind. A Vietnamese will often consider "What is best for my family?" when making a choice.

Sources of Anxiety Reduction

Vietnam's current transition to a market-oriented economy offers exciting opportunities for its citizens, but it also causes great anxieties. There are clear winners and losers. Vietnamese laborers in inefficient, state-owned industries know that they will be among the losers.

The extended family forms the basic unit of Vietnamese society and also provides the main source of security. Ancestor worship reinforces the importance of the family as well.

Issues of Equality/Inequality

Vietnam remains a hierarchical country. Under Confucian tradition, each person has a place and knows to whom to defer. Hierarchical structures are also found in government, business, and other organizations.

The ethnic Vietnamese have traditionally looked down upon the country's ethnic minorities. The rural minorities, such as the Montagnards (mountain people), have often reinforced Vietnamese stereotypes by trying to remain separate from mainstream Vietnamese society.

The Communist ideal includes gender equality, and women have equal rights under the law. However, Vietnam is still a male-dominated country, both in business and government. In most ethnic groups, the husband remains the titular head of the home. The aged are considered more knowledgeable than the young, and their opinions are highly respected.

▶ BUSINESS PRACTICES

Punctuality, Appointments, and Local Time

- Official business hours are generally from 7:00 or 7:30 A.M. to 4:30 or 5:00 P.M., Monday through Friday. Many people take a long lunch break.
- Punctuality is key; be on time for all business engagements.
- Being prompt is not as vital for social events, but do not be more than a half-hour late.

- In Vietnam, as in most other countries, the day is written first, then the month, then the year (e.g. December 3, 2010, is written 3.12.10).
- Prior appointments are necessary; do not try to make an impromptu office visit.
- The country of Vietnam is seven hours ahead of Greenwich Mean Time (G.M.T. + 7), or thirteen hours ahead of U.S. Eastern Standard Time (E.S.T. + 13).

Negotiating

- The Vietnamese are great fans of bargaining. They dicker over the price of everything, from taxi rides to real estate. When you finally get around to talking about the price, expect them to negotiate aggressively.
- Connections are all-important in Vietnam. You cannot do anything unless you are know the right (that is, powerful) people. Personal introductions are preferred, but a letter of introduction is better than nothing.
- The Vietnamese need to personally trust you before they will do business with you. Expect to spend a substantial amount of time exchanging small talk, drinking tea, and developing a rapport. Do not consider this time wasted.
- In common with other Asian cultures, the Vietnamese will often say what they believe foreigners want to hear. It is your job to learn to tell the difference between honest agreement and a polite-but-insincere "yes."
- High pressure and emotion have little place in business in Vietnam. Most would rather let a deal fall through than be rushed.

Business Entertaining

- Your Vietnamese host will give at least one meal in your honor. You should return the favor by hosting a meal at an international hotel or fine restaurant.
- Business meetings are often held over lunch. Dinners are usually considered social occasions, but work can be discussed—if your Vietnamese counterpart initiates the topic.

- Expect beer or spirits to be served at a Vietnamese banquet. The senior member of your party will be expected to make a short speech—or, at least, a toast.
- Karaoke has become very popular in Vietnam. It is worthwhile to prepare a song if you are asked to sing.
- If you happen to visit a Vietnamese kitchen, you will probably find it decorated with the images of three Vietnamese kitchen gods.
- Vietnam is becoming a destination for culinary travelers. The Vietnamese have learned to make food out of virtually every non-poisonous fish, beast, and plant native to their country. However, for those who are gastronomically timid, there are other cuisines available in Vietnam. In addition to Chinese and Thai food, Vietnamese cities have restaurants serving French and American cuisine. One can spend a considerable amount of time in Vietnam eating nothing but hamburgers and pizza.
- If you are a beer aficionado, you might want to visit one of the enormous beer halls that serve Bia Hoi (fresh beer)—brewed and served the same day.

Cultural Note

As a developing country, Vietnam boasts a small number of entertainment venues. After the workday, the legal forms of entertainment consist of karaoke, traditional arts performances, such as music, dance, water puppets—or drinking. While the Vietnamese are usually happy to welcome foreigners into their bars and beer gardens, keep in mind that they have a number of drinking games. You're in trouble when a Vietnamese shouts *"tram van tram,"* which means "100 percent!" You are now in a race with the challenger to drain your drink! Of course, as soon as you drain that one, several more Vietnamese will undoubtedly challenge you again.

▶ PROTOCOL

Greetings

- The traditional greeting is a slight bow with the hands clasped together above the waist. There is no physical contact. However, the vast majority of businesspeople in Vietnam will greet you with either a slight bow or a handshake.

- It is not traditional for Vietnamese to introduce themselves, and their subordinates will often not introduce their boss, either. This is one reason that a personal introduction is extremely useful in Vietnam—from a person considered more or less an equal.
- Good topics of conversation are sports, travel, food, and music.
- If a Vietnamese superstition is discussed, take it seriously. There are many Vietnamese who will give it credence, and your host may be one.
- Most (but not all) businesspeople have business cards. There is little formality involved in exchanging cards.
- Your card will not be refused, but you might not be given one in exchange. Don't be offended by this.

Titles/Forms of Address

- Vietnamese names are written in this order: surname (a.k.a., family name) followed by two given names.
- It is very important to use professional and governmental titles.

Cultural Note

Vietnam is noted for its unique musical instruments. The *Dan Bau* is an instrument that uses a single long string made of silk or brass. Vietnamese find its sound sublime, although it is so faint that it must be electronically amplified to be heard by even a small group of people. Other characteristic instruments include the bamboo flute, the *Tam Thap Luc* (a zither with thirty-six brass strings), and the gong.

Gestures

- In common with other Communist states, Vietnam is a relatively puritanical country. Although brief hugs or a kiss on the cheek are acceptable between friends, extended public contact between the sexes is frowned upon.
- In general, do not touch your Vietnamese associates at work. Allow for more physical distance than is normal in the West.
- The foot is considered unclean by many Vietnamese. Do not move anything with your feet, and do not touch anything (except the ground) with your feet.

- Do not show the soles of your feet (or shoes). This restriction determines how one sits: you can cross your legs at the knee but not with one ankle on your knee. Also, do not prop your feet on anything not intended for feet, such as a desk.
- Among Vietnamese Muslims, the left hand is considered unclean. Try to favor your right hand over your left when you are among them.
- As in much of the world, to beckon someone you hold your hand out, palm downward, and make a scooping motion with the fingers. Beckoning someone with the palm up and wagging one finger—as in North America—can be construed as an insult.

Gifts

- Gifts are part of doing business in Vietnam. Come prepared with a gift for each participant on your first meeting. These gifts need not be expensive: pens, small electronics, and illustrated books of your home country are all acceptable gifts.
- A more expensive gift is expected to commemorate the successful conclusion of a business deal or your return to your home country.
- Gifts should be carefully wrapped. Currently, the old tradition of not opening a wrapped gift in the presence of the giver is fading away. Some Vietnamese will put a wrapped gift aside to open later; some will open it immediately. You should follow their suggestion as to when you open a gift.
- Avoid using wrapping paper that is primarily white or black. Both of these colors are associated with death and mourning.
- Always bring something when invited to a house. Wine, candy, or flowers are the traditional choices.

Dress

- Dress in Vietnam is fairly casual, although clothing should cover most of the body (despite the tropical heat).
- While Communist governments are often quite puritanical, the current government of Vietnam restored national beauty contests in 1992. The classic Vietnamese four-flap dress worn by the

everyone from schoolgirls to beauty pageant contestants is known
as the *ao dai*. Traditionally, the ao dai was only worn once a year,
during the Tet Festival.

Cultural Note

Modesty is a characteristic of Vietnamese culture. Consequently, bragging and hype are largely
alien to Vietnamese people, and they are apt to respond badly to pompous behavior.

Titles and Forms of Address in Asian Countries

THERE ARE MANY NAMING CONVENTIONS within *Kiss, Bow, or Shake Hands: Asia*—single names, compound names, patronymics, names read right to left or left to right, honorifics, etc. For efficiency's sake, if multiple countries use the same customs, we have tried to consolidate them here. Some of this data may be repeated in certain chapters.

Chinese Naming Conventions

- Chinese names are listed in a different order from Western names. Traditionally, each person received three characters from the Chinese language. The first was the family name (from the father), then a middle name (which used to be called a generational name—one for all the brothers and another for all the sisters in a family), and finally a given name—in that order. Historically, generational names could have been planned out by a family's ancestors, and served a great purpose across the generations.

- After the Cultural Revolution, generational names became less common, and were supplanted by individual middle names. For example, in 2006, the President of the People's Republic of China and General Secretary of the Communist Party of China, President Hu Jintao had the family name of Hu, a middle name of Jin, and a given name of Tao. (His name could also be rendered Hu Chin-t'ao.)

- Chinese wives do not generally take their husband's surnames, but instead maintain their maiden names. Although Westerners commonly address a married woman as "Mrs." plus her husband's family name, it is more appropriate to call her "Madam" plus her maiden family name. For example, Liu Yongqing (female) is married to Hu Jintao (male). While Westerners would probably call her Mrs. Hu, she is properly addressed as Madam Liu.

- For the sake of Western conventions, Chinese women sometimes use their husbands' last names.

- Similarly, many Chinese adopt English first names so that English speakers can have familiar-sounding names to identify them. Thus, Chang Wu Jiang may call himself Mr. Tony Chang. Others use their initials (Mr. T. J. Chang), which indicates that Chang is his surname. Another way that Chinese businesspeople may clarify their surnames is by underlining or capitalizing them in written correspondence.

- Chinese names can be rendered different ways in English, so do not be surprised by variations. Chinese may have two names, but more often have three names, and the most common variant is whether or not to hyphenate the final two names. For example, the first chief executive of Hong Kong was Tung Chee Hwa. His name could also be rendered Tung Chee-hwa, or even Tung Cheehwa. (As with most Chinese, his surname is listed first, so he would be referred to as "Mr. Tung.")

- If many Chinese seem to have similar names, it is because there are only about 400 different surnames in China! However, when these surnames are transcribed into English, there are several possible variations. For example, Wong, Wang, and Huang are all English versions of the same Chinese clan name.

- Most people you meet should be addressed with a title and their name. If a person does not have a professional title (President, Engineer, Doctor), simply use "Mr." or "Madam," "Mrs.," or "Miss," plus the name.

- The Chinese are sensitive to status, so you should use official titles such as "General," "Committee Member," or "Bureau Chief." Never call anyone "Comrade" unless you are a Communist also.

Arabic Naming Conventions

- Muslim names are usually derived from Arabic. Translating from Arabic to other alphabets is not an exact science. Arabic names may be spelled several different ways in English. For example, the founder of the Kingdom of Saudi Arabia was King Abdul-Aziz Al-Saud. However, his name is also rendered in English as King Abd-al-Aziz Al Saud. History books tend to render his name as King Ibn Saud.

- Arabic naming traditions are used in many Islamic countries outside of the Middle East—for example, Indonesia. In general, names are written in the same order as English names: title, given name, middle name (often a patronymic), and surname (family name). In 2005, the new ruler of Saudi Arabia was King Abdullah Bin-Abd-al-Aziz al Saud; his title was "King," his given name was Abdullah, bin Abd-al-Aziz is a patronymic meaning "son of Abd-Aziz," and al-Saud was his family name. (King Abdullah succeeded the late King Fahd in August of 2005.)

- Many Arab names have specific meanings (e.g., *Amal* means "Hope"), or they are from the Bible (*Ibrahiim* means "Abraham"), or they are based upon the name of God in Arabic. Abd or Abdul are not complete names in themselves; they simply mean "servant of." King Abdul-al-Aziz can be translated as "Servant of the Almighty."

- The term *bin* (sometimes spelled *ibn*) literally means "from" in Arabic, so it is not immediately apparent whether a name like bin Mubarak indicates "son of Mubarak" or "from the town of Mubarak." However, most Saudis use it as a patronymic.

- If an Arab's grandfather is (or was) a famous person, he sometimes adds his grandfather's name. Thus, Dr. Mahmoud bin Sultan bin Hamad Al Muqrin is "Dr. Mahmoud, son of Sultan, grandson of Hamad, of the House (family) of Muqrin."

- Westerners frequently mistake bin for the name Ben, short for Benjamin. Obviously, bin has no meaning by itself, and one cannot address a Saudi as bin.

- The female version of bin is *bint*. Thus, Princess Fatima bint Ibrahim al-Saud is Princess "Fatima, daughter of Ibrahim, of the house of Saud."

- Arabic women generally do not change their names after they marry.

- Another common naming convention is a given name first, then the father's given name second, followed by the family name.

- Most Saudis should be addressed by title and given name (e.g., Prince Khalil), just as you would address a member of the British aristocracy (e.g., Sir John). They can also be addressed as "Your Excellency." In writing, use their full name.

- In Saudi Arabia, the title "Sheikh" (pronounced "shake") is used by any important leader well versed in the Koran, or an individual worthy of great respect; it does not designate membership in the royal family.

- A Muslim male who has completed his pilgrimage to Mecca is addressed as *Haji*. A woman who has done so would be addressed as *Hajjah*. Note that these titles are not automatically conferred on spouses; they must be individually earned by making the pilgrimage. However, when in doubt, err on the side of generosity. It is better to give a superfluous title than to omit one.

Indian Naming Conventions

- India's naming conventions are changing. For example, the southern region of India seems to be gradually moving toward the naming customs of the north, and professional females are starting to keep their maiden names.

- Titles are highly valued by Indians. Always use professional titles, such as "Professor" and "Doctor." Do not address someone by his or her first name unless you are asked to do so, or you are close friends; use "Mr.," "Mrs.," or "Miss." (In Hindi, "Mr." is *Shri* and "Mrs." is *Shrimati*.)

- Status is determined by the following: age, university degrees, caste, and profession.

- Hindus in the Northern region of India generally have a given name, a middle name, and a family name—written in that order. Female siblings may share a middle name, as may male siblings.

- Because one's name can indicate a caste, Northern Indian families sometimes opt to change their surnames.

- In the southern region, naming conventions differ. Traditionally, Hindus did not have family surnames. A Hindu Indian male may have used the initial of his father's name first, or the town he came from, followed by his own personal name. For example, V. Thiruselvan is "Thiruselvan, son of 'V.'" For legal purposes, both names would be written out with an *s/o* (for "son of") between the names: Thiruselvan s/o Vijay. In either case, he would be known as Mr. Thiruselvan. However, long Indian names are often shortened. He may prefer to be called either Mr. Thiru or Mr. Selvan.

- Hindu female names follow the same pattern: father's initial plus personal name. When fully written out, *d/o* (for "daughter of") is used instead of s/o. When an Indian woman married, she usually ceased to use her father's initial; instead, she followed her personal name with her husband's name. For instance, when S. Kamala (female) married V. Thiru (male), she might go by Mrs. Kamala Thiru.

- Some Indians will use Western-style surnames. Christian Indians may have biblical surnames like Abraham or Jacob. Indians from the former Portuguese colony of Goa may have surnames of Portuguese origin, such as Rozario or DeSilva. Such a person could be addressed as Dr. Jacob or Mr. DeSilva.

- Indian Sikhs generally have a given name followed by either *Singh* (for men) or *Kaur* (for women). Always address them by a title and first name. While Singh literally means "lion," to refer to a Sikh male as Mr. Singh may be as meaningless as saying "Mr. Man" in English.

Further data on naming conventions can be found on our Web site, *www.kissboworshakehands.com*, or in *Merriam Webster's Guide to International Business Communications*.

Why Learn a Foreign Language?

THROUGHOUT EUROPE, ASIA, and much of the world, business travelers are frequently multilingual. Their study of foreign languages begins in primary school, and often continues far into adulthood. Why do they study so hard to learn an unfamiliar tongue?

U.S. executives generally assume that foreigners learn English because it is the universal language of business. English has commonly predominated in business transactions for years, but that does not explain why German, Japanese, and Finnish executives expend substantial time and effort to learn Spanish, Mandarin, or Tamil.

The reason these business travelers study is to expand their trade in areas of the world such as Latin America, Asia, and the Indian subcontinent. And they understand that, in much of the world, business is built upon relationships. Speaking with prospects in their own language demonstrates a great deal of respect for that culture—it establishes a level of credibility for that executive, it builds trust, and it bridges the cultural gap.

Furthermore, many international executives are exceedingly self-reliant. They do not like depending upon interpreters. They resent missing out on various aspects of conversations, and they want clients to look at *them*—not the interpreters. So, frequent flyers from France, Austria, and Korea dedicate years to learning languages. And their clients respond.

Learning a country's language—and its regional dialects, accents, and vocabulary—gives one a deeper understanding of its culture. For example, when several French businessmen who had spoken perfect "British English" for twenty years were given new assignments in the Midwestern region of the USA, they started taking customized courses in "American-style English." Why? Because their Midwestern bosses thought that their English was "too Euro." Their "American English" training included television shows that reflected current U.S. cultural styles—like *The Apprentice*. It also taught them how to communicate in sound bites, write in bullet format, and pepper their communications with sports analogies. Just like their U.S. bosses.

But what if you do not have a background in languages, and want to begin learning the most widely spoken language on earth—Mandarin? Numerous multinationals now realize they will require employees who are fluent in Mandarin, and they are initiating programs to build their own multilingual workforces.

Bettina Anagnostopoulos, Manager of Language Projects at Cartus *(www.cartus.com)*, has been involved in this process for years. She has designed many projects, including a "Seven Level Mandarin" program at a corporate university in California. The training is not just for "high potentials" who are being considered for assignments in China, but also for non-traveling virtual team members, business travelers, and others who may be offered Asian assignments in the future. The program includes various courses, from "Beginner Chinese for Heritage Learners" (these are employees with Chinese parents, or those who grew up in China), to "Advanced Business Chinese," which includes accent modification for Chinese-Americans who need to adjust their pronunciation and inflections in order to communicate effectively with native Chinese. One interesting aspect of the "sustained training" that Cartus recommends is that it must be stimulating enough to motivate learners beyond their second or third year. The program integrates "Cultural Mentors" (or coaches) with language teachers, electronic training, videos, music, podcasts, and other personalized learning methods.

Of course, the best option for absorbing a language is still a formal educational program, starting at a young age. The USA is slowly catching on to the importance of teaching Chinese in public schools, and hopefully will soon implement programs like Seattle, Washington's twelve-year curriculum in Mandarin.

Besides formal educational programs and corporate training resources, you can find scores of language and translation options on the Web. A search on "foreign phrases" or "foreign language learn-ing" will generate any number of products. As a start, try the British Broadcasting Corporation's Web site for languages at *www.bbc.co.uk/ languages*. Other links for foreign language programs and translation systems are available at *www.kissboworshakehands.com*.

Considering the kinetics of world demographics, English may not be the sole language of business in the decades to come. Be ahead of the curve, and *buon viaggio*!

"Una persona que habla dos lenguas vale dos personas."
A person who speaks two languages is worth two people.
—SPANISH PROVERB

Appendix C

Contacts and Resources

BECAUSE OF THE DYNAMIC NATURE of travel warnings, customs requirements, and so on, this section directs you to several large Web sites that provide broad-based, helpful data for international travelers. While every country has its own respective requirements, the U.S. Web sites included here are a reasonable start for international business contacts, travel advisories, medical information, passports, etc.

Government Sites

Make it a practice to contact your country's embassy when you travel, as it can prove helpful in emergency situations. Many embassies now allow registration of your information online.

Embassies can arrange appointments with local business and government officials; provide counsel on local trade regulations, laws, and customs; and identify importers, buyers, agents, etc. They may also provide economic, political, technological, and labor data. There are many lists of embassies on the Web, such as *http://usembassy .state.gov*. Other helpful government sites include:

www.state.gov/travel
This site provides:
- Travel warnings
- Consular information sheets
- Public announcements
- Passports and visas for U.S. citizens
- Country background notes

- Foreign consular offices in the United States
- Key officers at U.S. foreign service posts

www.customs.ustreas.gov
Produces a database that can be queried by topic, (e.g., travel requirements, importing procedures, etc.), or an individual's status (e.g., importer, traveler, carrier, etc.)

www.cia.gov
The U.S. Central Intelligence Agency produces several documents of note for global travelers. These include:
- The World Factbook (at *www.cia.gov/cia/publications/factbook*)
- An online directory called "The Chiefs of State and Cabinet Members of Foreign Governments," available at *www.cia .gov/cia/publications/chiefs/index.html.* This informational directory is updated weekly and includes many governments of the world, including some with which the United States of America has no diplomatic exchanges, and which are not officially recognized.

Corruption and Bribery
www.transparency.org
Transparency International, a worldwide nongovernmental organization, reports on corruption and bribery around the world. They issue an annual "Corruption Perceptions_Index," which relates to perceptions of the degree of corruption as seen by businesspeople, academics, and risk analysts. In the "2005 Corruption Perceptions Index," the five least corrupt countries out of 158 were Iceland (number 1), Finland, New Zealand, Denmark, and Singapore. The five most highly corrupt were Haiti, Myanmar, Turkmenistan, Bangladesh, and Chad (number 158).

Medical Information
www.cdc.gov/travel
The Centers for Disease Control provides an abundance of medical resources for international travelers. It includes everything

from health information and vaccinations required for specific destinations, to advice on traveling with children and pets.

Of course, you will want to be thoroughly prepared for your trip, so schedule physical and dental examinations well before leaving. Remember that some vaccinations must be given over a period of time. Also take current medical documentation with you, and list any chronic conditions and current prescription drugs (including dosages). In order to avoid problems at customs, carry all medications in their original containers. Also, take an extra set of glasses, contacts, or prescriptions. In your bags, include the name, address, and phone number of someone to be contacted in case of an emergency.

Prepare a basic medical travel kit, which might include aspirin, a topical antibiotic, bandages, a disinfectant, 0.5 percent hydrocortisone cream (for bites or sunburn), sunblock, a thermometer, and diarrhea medication. Pack the kit in your carry-on luggage (if you are permitted a carry-on bag!).

Also confirm that you have sufficient travel medical insurance. There are two main types of travel insurance: 1) policies that make direct payments for medical care and provide assistance, and 2) policies that reimburse you for emergency expenses. (With the latter option, you might have to pay the doctor or hospital immediately—in local currency—and file a claim once you return home.)

While we do not endorse any specific organizations, the Bureau of Consular Affairs maintains an extensive list of Travel Insurance Companies, as well as Air Ambulance, Med-Evac companies, and Executive Medical Services. A list of these firms is available at *http://travel.state.gov/travel/tips/health/health_1185.html.*

Appendix D

Avoiding Fashion Faux Pas

"Dressing for Success" can vary from country to country. One person's power suit is another's poor taste, and none of us want to distract potential clients with our wild attire.

Even mistakes in your accessories can be highly detrimental to a prospective sale. For example, there's the story of the Texan and the Italian in Chile. A large Chilean firm was nearing the end of a contract-evaluation process for oilfield equipment. The Texan and Italian CEOs both had bids in on the contract; both wanted the job. When the final negotiations approached, the president of the Chilean firm asked to meet the short-list bidders before making his decision.

The CEO from Texas arrived for his meeting in Santiago wearing an expensive light-gray suit. His jewelry a designer watch, a heavy gold ring from his alma mater, a massive silver belt buckle, and a pair of snakeskin boots. When the Italian arrived, he wore a dark, well-fitted suit, a subtle tie, and was devoid of jewelry. Although the U.S. company actually had a broader line of products, the Chilean awarded the contract to the Italian firm, and explains that "the U.S. company's products may have been nominally better than the Italian's, but I needed to trust the CEO of the company I was going to work with. The ostentatious show of jewelry and the loud clothes on the U.S. CEO indicated to me that he was in business to amass personal wealth and had the poor judgment to show it."

Chileans generally opt for more conservative clothing. Bright colors and flashy fashions are not suitable, nor are eye-catching accessories (lapel pins, etc.).

Obviously, rules of correct attire vary from country to country. What is in good taste in Dallas may be totally wrong in Dubai or

Delhi. If you are traveling to any of the following Asian destinations, consider the following cultural guidelines and try to outfit yourself aptly for each country.

- *China:* Even casual wear is somewhat conservative. Revealing clothing in a business environment may be offensive. In social situations, jeans are acceptable for both men and women.
- *Japan:* Never appear casual at work. Slip-on shoes are best, because you remove them frequently. Tall women should eschew extremely high heels to avoid towering over their Japanese counterparts.
- *India:* Remember that some Hindus consider leather products offensive (especially in temples). While many Hindus are very tolerant of others' beliefs, it is prudent to leave most of your finely tooled leather belts, wallets, boots, and briefcases at home, and invest in some high-quality fabric accessories.

In some countries, men remove their jackets at work, while in other countries, executives usually do not loosen their ties or take off their jackets while at the office. Never be the first to shed your jacket.

Colors of clothing can have significant meaning around the world. Some hues and patterns can set the wrong tone in certain locations:

- *Yellow* is associated with illness in South Korea, and certain shades of yellow are reserved for the royal families to wear in Malaysia.
- *White* is a color of mourning in much of Asia.
- *Green* hats (like the famous "John Deere" signature caps) carry the connotation that you are a cuckold (your wife is cheating on you) in certain parts of Asia. Don't hand them out at exhibitions or conferences!

In general, bright, vivid colors are not a good choice for business apparel in any country. Your garments form a large part of people's first impressions of you, so investing in suitable attire will allow your clients to spend more time listening to what you say, rather than looking at what you wear.

APPENDIX E

Holidays

EVERY COUNTRY IN THE WORLD celebrates holidays, and little or no work is conducted during these celebrations. However, holidays are always subject to change. Governments frequently add, delete, or move certain official holidays. Furthermore, the dates for many holidays do not fall on the same day in the Western (Gregorian) calendar each year. This may be because they are dated using a calendar that does not correspond to the Western calendar (for example, the Arabic Hijra calendar is lunar, and is only 354 days long).

Some cultures use lunisolar calendars (for instance, the Hebrew and Chinese calendars—although these two are not similar in other aspects), and some have both the aspects of solar and lunisolar calendars (for example, the Hindu calendar).

Actually, there are over twenty calendars in use around the world! Indonesia is a good example of one country that uses multiple calendars. They include the Gregorian calendar, one which is similar to the Islamic calendar, a calendar used primarily in Java, and several others. In Java, when the fifth day of a month coincides on all the calendars various celebrations take place (businesses are opened, babies are named, etc.). This is because five is an auspicious number—there are five sacred mountains, five elements, and so forth.

Some holidays are purposefully consecutive, like "Golden Week" in Japan. It allows for Japanese workers to enjoy extended vacations and observe some important holidays together.

The work week may be different in various cultures as well. For example, in the Muslim world, the Sabbath is celebrated on Friday. Some Islamic nations have their "weekend" on Thursday and Friday, and their work week runs Saturday through Wednesday.

Whatever the calendar or work week in use, the only way to be sure your business trip is not interrupted by official or local holidays is to contact reliable, up-to-date sources before your trip. Consult with the country's embassy, call your associates at your destination, or reference our World Holiday Guide at: *www.kissboworshakehands.com*.

One additional note: You may see the traditional terms B.C. (before Christ) and A.D. (anno Domini, "the year of the Lord") being used interchangeably or replaced with the terms B.C.E. (before the Common Era) and C.E. (Common Era). The new notation "Common" refers to the most common calendar—the Gregorian, or Western Calendar.

Appendix F

Equivalents

Unit	Metric Equivalent	U.S. Equivalent
acre	0.404 685 64 hectares	43,560 feet^2
acre	4,046,856 4 meters^2	4,840 yards^2
acre	0.004 046 856 4 kilometers^2	0.001 562 5 miles^2, statute
acre	100 meters^2	119.599 yards^2
barrel (petroleum, U.S.)	158.987 29 liters	42 gallons
(proof spirits, U.S.)	151.416 47 liters	40 gallons
(beer, U.S.)	117.347 77 liters	31 gallons
bushel	35.239 07 liters	4 pecks
cable	219.456 meters	120 fathoms
chain (surveyor's)	20.116 8 meters	66 feet
cord (wood)	3.624 556 meters^3	128 feet^3
cup	0.236 588 2 liters	8 ounces, liquid (U.S.)
degrees, Celsius	(water boils at 100°C, freezes at 0°C)	multiply by 1.8 and add 32 to obtain °F
degrees, Fahrenheit	subtract 32 and divide by 1.8 to obtain C°	(water boils at 212°F, freezes at 32°F)
dram, avoirdupois	1.771 845 2 grams	0.0625 5 ounces, avoirdupois
dram, troy	3.887 934 6 grams	0.125 ounces, troy
dram, liquid (U.S.)	3.696 69 milliliters	0.125 ounces, liquid
fathom	1.828 8 meters	6 feet
foot	30.48 centimeters	12 inches
foot	0.304 8 meters	0.333 333 3 yards
foot	0.000 304 8 kilometers	0.000 189 39 miles, statute
foot^2	929.030 4 centimeters^2	144 inches^2

Unit	Metric Equivalent	U.S. Equivalent
foot	20.092 903 04 meters^2	0.111 111 1 yards^2
foot^3	28.316 846 592 liters	7.480 519 gallons
foot^3	0.028 316 847 meters^3	1,728 inches^3
furlong	201.168 meters	220 yards
gallon, liquid (U.S.)	3.785 411 784 liters	4 quarts, liquid
gill (U.S.)	118.294 118 milliliters	4 ounces, liquid
grain	64.798 91 milligrams	0.002 285 71 ounces, avdp.
gram	1,000 milligrams	0.035 273 96 ounces, avdp.
hand (height of horse)	10.16 centimeters	4 inches
hectare	10,000 meters^2	2.471 053 8 acres
hundredweight, long	50.802 345 kilograms	112 pounds, avoirdupois
hundredweight, short	45.359 237 kilograms	100 pounds, avoirdupois
inch	2.54 centimeters	0.083 333 33 feet
inch^2	6.451 6 centimeters^2	0.006 944 44 feet^2
inch^3	16.387 064 milliliters	0.000 578 7 feet^3
inch^3	16.387 064 milliliters	0.029 761 6 pints, dry
inch^3	16.387.064 milliliters	0.034 632 0 pints, liquid
kilogram	0.001 tons, metric	2.204 626 pounds, avoirdupois
kilometer	1,000 meters	0.621 371 19 miles, statue
kilometer^2	100 hectares	247.105 38 acres
kilometer^2	1,000,000 meters^2	0.386 102 16 miles^2, statue
knot (1 nautical mi/hr)	1.852 kilometers/hour	1.151 statue miles/hour
league, nautical	5.559 552 kilometers	3 miles, nautical
league, statute	4.828 032 kilometers	3 miles, statute
link (surveyor's)	20.116 8 centimeters	7.92 inches
liter	0.001 meters^3	61.023 74 inches^3
liter	0.1 dekaliter	0.908 083 quarts, dry
liter	1,000 milliliters	1.056 688 quarts, liquid

Unit	Metric Equivalent	U.S. Equivalent
meter	100 centimeters	1.093 613 yards
meter^2	10,000 centimeters^2	1.195 990 yards^2
meter^3	1,000 liters	1.307 951 yards^3
micron	0.000 001 meter	0.000 039 4 inches
mil	0.025 4 millimeters	0.001 inch
mile, nautical	1.852 kilometers	1.150 779 4 miles, statute
mile^2, nautical	3.429 904 kilometers^2	1.325 miles^2, statute
mile, statute	1.609 344 kilometers	5,280 feet or 8 furlongs
mile^2, statute	258.998 811 hectares	640 acres or 1 section
mile^2, statute	2.589 988 11 kilometers^2	0.755 miles^2, nautical
minim (U.S.)	0.061 611 52 milliliters	0.002 083 33 ounces, liquid
ounce, avoirdupois	28.349 523 125 grams	437.5 grains
ounce, liquid (U.S.)	29.573 53 milliliters	0.062 5 pints, liquid
ounce, troy	31.103 476 8 grams	480 grains
pace	76.2 centimeters	30 inches
peck	8.809 767 5 liters	8 quarts, dry
pennyweight	1.555 173 84 grams	24 grains
pint, dry (U.S.)	0.550 610 47 liters	0.5 quarts, dry
pint, liquid (U.S.)	0.473 176 473	0.5 quarts, liquid
point (typographical)	0.351 459 8 milliliters	0.013 837 inches
pound, avoirdupois	453.592 37 grams	16 ounces, avoirdupois
pound, troy	373.241 721 6 grams	12 ounces, troy
quart, dry (U.S.)	1.101 221 liters	2 pints, dry
quart, liquid (U.S.)	0.946 352 946 liters	2 pints, liquid
quintal	100 kilograms	220.462 26 pounds, avdp.
rod	5.029 2 meters	505 yards
scruple	1.295 978 2 grams	20 grains
section (U.S.)	2.589 988 1 kilometers^2	1 mile^2, statute or 640 acres

Unit	Metric Equivalent	U.S. Equivalent
span	22.86 centimeters	9 inches
stere	1 meter^3	1.307 95 yards^3
tablespoon	14.786 76 milliliters	3 teaspoons
teaspoon	4.928 922 milliliters	0.333 333 tablespoons
ton, long or deadweight	1,016.046.909 kilograms	2,240 pounds, avoirdupois
ton, metric	1,000 kilograms	2,204.623 pounds, avoirdupois
ton, register	2.831 684 7 meters^3	100 feet^3
ton, short	907.184 74 kilograms	2,000 pounds, avoirdupois
township (U.S.)	93.239 572 kilometers^2	36 miles^2, statute
yard	0.914 4 meters	3 feet
yard^2	0.836 127 36 meters^2	9 feet^2
yard^3	0.764 554 86 meters^3	27 feet^3
yard^3	764.554 857 984 liters	201.974 gallons

Appendix G

International Electrical Adaptors

This data is excerpted from a publication of the U.S. Department of Commerce.

The electricity used in much of the world (220–250 volts) is a different voltage from that used in North America (110–125 volts). Electrical appliances designed for North America may need converters to "step down" this higher voltage to the level required to operate. Some appliances cannot be converted for use elsewhere because they require sixty cycles per second (again, found primarily in North America), or they may have other requirements. Electrical wall sockets found around the world are also likely to differ in shape from the sockets used in North America. Electrical adaptor plugs are available to slip over the plugs of North American appliances for use in such sockets.

The following table and illustrations will inform you about the types of plugs you may encounter in various Asian and Pacific countries.

Type of Plug by Country

Country Plug	Type	Country Plug	Type
Bangladesh	A, C, D	Malaysia	G
Burma	C, D, F	Nepal	C, D
Brunei	G	Pakistan	B, C, D
China, Peoples Rep. of	C, D, G, H	Philippines	A, B, C
Fiji	I	Singapore	B, H
Hong Kong	H	Sri Lanka	D
India	C, D, G	Tahiti	A
Indonesia	C, E, F	Taiwan	A, B
Japan	A, B, I	Thailand	A, B, C, D, E, G, J, K
Korea	C	Western Samoa	H
Laos	A, B, C, E, F		

Plugs in Commercial Use

Type A Flat blade attachment plug	**Type B** Flat blades with round grounding pin
Type C Round pin attachment plug	**Type D** Round pins with ground
Type E Round pin plug and receptacle with male grounding pin	**Type F** "Schuko" plug and receptacle with side grounding contacts
Type G Rectangular blade plug	**Type H** Oblique flat blades with ground
Type I Oblique flat blade with ground	**Type J** Round pins with ground
Type K Round pins with ground	**Type L** Round pins with ground

Index

About the Authors

TERRI MORRISON and WAYNE A. CONAWAY have coauthored five books on intercultural communications, hundreds of articles, and several databases—all of which are available at *www.kissboworshake hands.com*. Terri Morrison also offers keynote seminars on intercultural communications, which range from one to three hours. These highly informative, entertaining, and interactive presentations can be customized for specific industries, countries, and regions of the world. A speaker video, biography, and references are available at *www.TerriMorrison.com*.

Their electronic product *Kiss, Bow, or Shake Hands: Expanded Edition* (KBSH:XE) contains up-to-date business and cultural data on over 100 countries. Numerous private and public institutions have found KBSH:XE to be a valuable tool for facilitating globalization. Subscriptions are available for corporate, educational, governmental, and personal usage, and contain information on everything from Business Practices (appointments, negotiating, entertaining, etc.) to Intellectual Property Rights and Culturally-Correct Gifts. A demo of KBSH:XE is available at their Web site.

The electronic *World Holiday and Time Zone Guide* contains a useful format of cross-referencing holidays both by the country and by the day of the year. This database is a convenient feature for heavy travelers, meeting planners, and researchers who need current holiday information on 101 countries.

The study of intercultural communication represents a lifelong interest for the authors of *Kiss, Bow, or Shake Hands*. By way of continuing that research, the authors invite your comments. Whether your own experience confirms or diverges from the data in this book, they welcome your perspective. Please contact them at:

TerriMorrison@getcustoms.com
Phone: 610-725-1040

Or via these Web sites:

www.getcustoms.com
www.TerriMorrison.com
www.kissboworshakehands.com

> *Virtue is bold, and goodness never fearful.*
> —William Shakespeare